FRUIT AND VEGGIES 101 - SALAD VEGETABLES

GARDENING GUIDE ON HOW TO GROW THE FRESHEST & RIPEST SALAD VEGETABLES (PERFECT FOR BEGINNERS)

GREEN ROOTS

Fruit **and** Veggies **101**

SALAD VEGETABLES

Gardening Guide On How To Grow The Freshest & Ripest Salad Vegetables

(Perfect For Beginners)

GREEN ROOTS

CONTENTS

A SPECIAL GIFT TO OUR READERS

Included with your purchase of this book is our list of "27 horticulture Myths Debunked"
This list will provide and aid you as a new (or soon-to-be) gardener by actively informing you of the myths and irrelevant practices to avoid during your gardening journey.

Visit the link below to let us know which email address to deliver to

www.gardengreenroots.com

INTRODUCTION

Did you know that spending time in nature can have an incredibly positive effect on your mental health? Research proves that just 10 minutes in the garden can lift your spirits and help change your mindset from negative to positive. But the benefits don't stop there. Spending quality time in nature also lowers blood pressure and heart rate.

Furthermore for seniors, gardening and time outdoors can even boost positive aging effects (Scott et al., 2014). Imagine feeling an immediate mood boost from simply looking at trees, gardening, or taking a walk in the park. It's truly incredible and it's a pleasure to welcome you to join the many others who have experienced the power of nature on their mental wellbeing.

RECLAIM AND REVITALIZE YOUR WELL-BEING WITH GARDENING

Life may feel complex, confusing, and uncertain at times. These are feelings that are commonly experienced by the majority across all genders and races. With how intense life can get, it is very easy to forget one of the most important things you should prioritize; your well-being.

You are not alone. We can relate to this life experience, and many others can. It is far from something to be ashamed of, as it's simply life's journey.

This guide is precisely what you need in situations where you feel unproductive, lonely, or not in the best of mental spaces. Why? Because with 20 years of collective gardening experience, we have seen and experienced first-hand how powerful gardening can be. We have seen lives transformed and changed by learning how to plant for themselves.

I'm sure you may have heard or come across the term "Hiding in plain sight". We believe this term perfectly explains one of the most underrated or underestimated methods when prioritizing and looking after your well-being; this is via the art of gardening.

You might be wondering how you can start gardening and reap the benefits of fresh produce and the wonderful health benefits of this amazing hobby.

Home gardening is used by many around the world for leisure purposes and for some as a way to provide for their families. Although gardening is relaxing, it brings benefits beyond the physical produces. It can contribute significantly to physical health, as you can eat a healthier diet due to having vegetables readily available in your garden, to be picked, washed, and consumed, and the best part is that it will cost you less than what it costs at a store.

We all wish we could have ultimate control over our health, lifestyle, and well-being. Well gardening provides you with that control. From being able to grow the types of food you wish to consume, physically getting fitter and at the same time enjoying the relaxed and peaceful environment you've created.

Imagine having complete control over the nutrients in your soil, the environment of your garden, and the quality of water your plants consume. Even better, what if you could avoid all the dangerous pesticides and chemicals used on most commercially produced vegetables and enjoy the satisfaction of achieving an organic lifestyle.

What if you could find a hobby and a great mechanism to strengthen your daily mental health? We are positive that with this guide this can be achieved along will an array of lifestyle benefits.

What You Can Expect to Learn

In this guide, you will learn all there is to know about gardening for vegetables. Our beginner-friendly guide provides a comprehensive overview of vegetable gardening, without any unnecessary fluff.

Each chapter is packed with practical tips and actionable steps to help you start your own vegetable garden right at home. From preparing your gardening space to cultivating a bountiful harvest, our guide has everything you need to become a gardening expert.

The vegetables you will learn to plant and grow successfully are tomatoes, cucumbers, cabbages, carrots, peppers, spring onions, and radishes.

Why This Book Is Exactly What You Need

You may question whether this is the right book to guide you into vegetable gardening. We're happy to say it is because we have injected 20 years of collective gardening knowledge and experience into this book.

We will show you all the successful tips and tricks we have used over the years, especially those we have used to maintain gardens long term.

There are so many misconceptions and myths about gardening—that you need specific tools (some of which are expensive), that you need lots of space that you may not have, and that only people who are gifted with gardeners' hands can grow healthy nutritious vegetables.

We will not only dispel these myths, but we will teach you how to make the most of the space and tools you have to grow your garden. If you don't have special and gifted gardeners' hands, don't worry. Successful gardeners are not born but made through teaching, learning, and implementation. Most importantly, gardeners are made by learning from those who have planted before them.

You took the first steps to becoming a successful gardener, and you will achieve great results with the knowledge we share in this book. You may have a garden already yet are feeling incredibly frustrated because it isn't turning out how you would have wanted it to.

Perhaps you want to start a vegetable garden but don't know where to begin and feel overwhelmed. We have not just worked on our vegetable gardens over the years, but we have helped other people start theirs and maintain them successfully.

You are in safe hands. This guide will support you throughout your gardening journey. Now, let the journey begin!

CHAPTER 1
YOUR GROWING SPACE: PREPARATION AND TECHNIQUES

Remember how we told you that there are various misconceptions and myths about growing your vegetable garden? Well, the same can be said about myths surrounding where one should grow their garden.

Many myths have caused many people to stop and rethink their decision to start their gardening journey. We hear a lot about how the older you get, the harder it is to learn new things, especially with hobbies, and that couldn't be further from the truth.

With the right tools and resources, you can achieve your goal of creating a garden that produces the kind of vegetables you want. The right knowledge and correct implementation will yield results—all you need to do is be open to learning and patient.

CHOOSE WHERE YOUR GARDEN WILL GROW

The first step in starting your vegetable garden is figuring out where you will grow your vegetables—the area or spot you will be planting. Most people not well versed in vegetable gardening only think of planting in the ground - however, there is more than one way to go about it.

To choose a suitable garden for your space, you will need to inspect your home and yard for what will work best for you. That's because your living environment and home will likely dictate the kind of garden you opt for. Not everyone will have enough room in their yards to plant, therefore other alternatives work best.

There are three most common ways to grow a vegetable garden: in-ground—the traditional way, in containers, or in raised beds. Each one of these may or may not work for your space or the kind of vegetables you want to grow. We will discuss each type of garden along with its pros and cons.

IN-GROUND GARDEN

This type of garden is considered traditional, the most adopted, allowing you to grow various vegetable plants. If you choose this garden type, your vegetable plants will be planted directly in the ground or soil.

Your in-ground garden will need a good amount of sun; as a result, ensure the area you choose to use has good sunlight exposure. You can do this by monitoring the sun and how the area you consider using is exposed enough for your plants to grow strong.

One of the pros of traditional gardening is that you will take advantage of the naturally occurring minerals in the soil. This may help you save money! Plus, you could avoid spending too much money on fertilizers.

Pros Of In-Ground Gardening

- You will only need to spend a little time setting it up or constructing it.
- You will have more space.
- Vegetable roots have enough space to grow as needed.
- It will cost less money to set it up.
- You can grow a large variety of vegetables.

Cons Of In-Ground Gardening

- The soil may get too bulky and dense, causing slow water drainage.
- There is a chance of possible slowed plant growth due to soil compaction.
- If soil quality is terrible, it may require a lot of investment to create healthy soil.
- Possible weed and insect infestations may occur.
- Soil quality can be challenging to control.

CONTAINER GARDEN

If you don't have good soil and prefer not to treat your soil as it can be costly financially, container gardening might be for you. This type of garden is one where plants are grown from containers such as clay pots.

Various gardeners use containers to plant herbs and smaller or less demanding vegetables like parsley. This type of garden may be a good option if you do not have enough space for the traditional kind of garden.

Pros Of Container Gardening

- You can buy good and treated soil ready to use for containers.
- It's easy to set up.
- Containers can be movable in most cases.
- Containers can also be moved around to access adequate sunlight.
- There's virtually no weed infestation.
- There are fewer chances of soil compaction.
- A great option for easy water drainage.
- You can control the quality of your soil.

Cons Of Container Gardening

- It takes a decent financial investment to start.
- Roots can be compressed with little space to grow.
- Roots can rot if not properly cared for.

RAISED BED GARDEN

This type of garden can confuse many, as it's not always understood. It can seem like a hybrid between traditional in-ground gardening and container gardening.

A raised bed garden is essentially very much like a container garden. It's typically stationary and on the ground level; however, the soil is enclosed and above the ground level.

Although they are typically around eight inches to three feet in height, raised beds can be as high as you need them to be. Due to the nature of raised bed gardens, it's essential to ensure that water drainage is not a problem, especially on the bottom surface.

This type of garden will need space; therefore, this is something you will need to make sure you have before starting it. This is also a great choice for those unable to utilize a traditional garden due to physical limitations.

Pros Of Raised Bed Gardening

- With pre-made raised beds, it can be easy to set up.
- There's virtually no weed infestation.
- There are fewer chances of soil compaction.
- A great option for easy water drainage.
- You can control the quality of your soil.
- Suitable for those with physical limitations.
- Suitable for people with back problems.

Cons Of Raised Bed Gardening

- It can be time-consuming and tedious to set up if the raised beds are a DIY project.
- There are financial expenses to start or set up.
- They can't be moved around like containers.

If you cannot choose any of the three gardens for your home and feel a hybrid or combination may work, you can also do that. You can combine either two or all three to create a suitable garden for your vegetables.

BEGINNER ESSENTIALS TOOLS AND EQUIPMENT

Now that you have established the kind of garden you want to start, we will share with you the tools you will need to not only begin a garden but maintain it in the best way possible.

With the long list of gardening tools in stores, you can easily become confused and uncertain about what to buy. However, we will make it very easy for you because the truth is you don't need a whole lot to begin with; plus, some are optional to grow a successful vegetable garden. As a beginner, gardening is already daunting, so we will save you time and trouble by sharing with you what you need.

BEGINNER GARDENING TOOLS

Pruning Shears

Pruning your vegetable plants is essential for their healthy growth and for maintaining a good environment for them to grow. Pruning shears are not only for beginners, but they are tools used by beginner, intermediate, and advanced gardeners.

The benefit of buying this tool earlier in your journey is that you will likely not need another one for quite some time. Once you have your pruning shears, you will need to monitor your vegetable plants and cut off parts that have dried up.

You can also use pruning shears to cut off parts of healthy vegetable plants to keep or make space for your other plants.

Garden Rake

You will need to keep the surface of your vegetable soil healthy. One of the ways to do this is to ensure that debris such as leaves does not cause harm by causing diseases or mold. When leaves, weeds, or other unwanted debris sits on your vegetables and the soil, it can prevent proper growth.

Therefore, the garden rake will help prevent these possible harmful situations. Furthermore, garden rakes are very useful in maintaining a certain look by keeping your vegetable garden clean and neat.

Raking can mark your soil and prepare you to plant your vegetable seeds. Some rakes are made especially for different purposes such as marking. Always be mindful of the force and technique you use when raking. It is possible to cause more harm than good.

Also, it would help if you explored the different garden rakes. For instance, some gardens do not need harsh raking but light raking. In this case, a plastic garden rake or a more delicate one may be helpful.

Garden Hand Trowel

Trowels are incredibly useful when you are planting your vegetables, digging up small to medium holes, and removing unwanted weeds. They are typically an excellent tool for container or raised bed gardens; however, they are also useful in in-ground gardens.

Therefore, this is a tool that will help you dig up holes and maintain your garden with ease, especially if you have a smaller garden. Garden trowels can be used with one hand; they are generally light and safe for people with back problems.

Garden Spade

A spade is also called a shovel, primarily used for digging deep and large holes. It's usually used for larger and more traditional in-ground gardens.

There are various types of spades that you can use in your garden—different sizes, different materials, and such. When choosing the best one for you, focusing on its design will save you disappointment. For example, a spade with a pointy head will help you minimize your effort in digging.

It will make it easier to get the job done, unlike others with square-shaped styles and slightly blunt. A spade is also useful in removing soil from one space to another or into a wheelbarrow. This tool is essential, and the best one for you will be determined by the kind of garden you have and what you are trying to achieve.

Garden Fork

A garden fork is a beneficial tool with compacted soil that needs more force to work through it. The traditional kind of garden fork is typically used for in-ground gardens.

However, it can come in different designs, weights, and materials. Garden forks are helpful when you need to dig out deep roots in the soil to soften the soil around your vegetable plants and reduce soil compaction.

It can help you transfer a whole plant from one area to another without damaging it. Be cautious when you use a garden fork, as it can hurt your plants and damage roots when misused.

Garden Hoe

Much like the garden rake, a garden hoe is useful in removing weeds, stones, or rocks and keeping your vegetable soil surface clean. You might think both a hoe and a rake are similar that you could do without one; however, they are both needed.

A garden hoe is more efficient in removing hard and challenging debris such as stone or rocks, whereas a rake may be less efficient.

Garden Hose

Deciding what watering method to use for your garden will depend on how large your garden space is, the number of vegetable plants, the water drainage your type of garden has, and whether or not you can exert the necessary effort to use that watering method.

A garden watering hose can be handheld or placed on the leveled ground to water your plants. Hoses are useful when you cannot use watering cans.

Using a hose may be a better choice if a person cannot carry the weight or has a physical limitation.

Watering Cans

For fragile and delicate vegetable plants, the use of watering cans is a smarter choice, especially for those with a gentle spray nozzle. You can use watering cans for containers, raised beds, and in-ground gardens.

The use of watering cans allows you to control the water nutrients and minerals for your vegetable plants. Should your plants need an extra boost of some minerals or wish to treat them for weeds, you can use the watering cans to do so successfully.

For those who find it challenging to carry a heavy load, a watering can may not be a good choice. Instead, a hose that has a gentle spray nozzle with a pressure you can control will work better.

Garden Gloves

The odds of needing to touch the soil, plants, and soil treatments are high. You may not be keen to touch any of them with your bare hands, especially if you are allergic to certain plants or compounds found in gardening.

Therefore, gloves are incredibly important to protect your hands from dirt, eggs, worms, and other issues.

Garden Wheelbarrow

To carry around your garden tools, plants, and soil, a wheelbarrow will come in very handy. Your garden might be far from all your essentials, and using a wheelbarrow will help you transport what you need without straining your back.

Although wheelbarrows allow you to carry more than you could with your bare hands, there are limits to their uses for those who generally cannot push heavy things.

Therefore, you might need to carry a lighter load or choose a garden location close to all your essentials.

Garden Trug

A trug is a tool you need to hold your vegetables when you are harvesting, and they are sold in different sizes and materials. It helps you make fewer trips to and from the house for storage.

All you do is carry it with you as you pick your vegetables from your lovely garden. This tool may seem meaningless, but it's essential to harvesting.

There are adjustments you can make to vegetable trugs to make them easy to carry around if you cannot handle the weight. You can have one attached to a cart or something similar to allow you to carry it around without hurting your back.

PREPARE YOUR SOIL: GARDEN SOIL 101

Soil to plants is like the air humans need to live and survive. Plants need soil—not just any kind of soil but healthy soil. It needs to be packed with all the necessary minerals to grow strong and nutritious vegetable plants.

It can be easy to assume that all soils are healthy; unfortunately, this is not the case. Different kinds of soil may or may not support life for all vegetable plants.

Some plants need a concentration of some minerals to grow a certain way and some do not. Some vegetable plants can grow in lousy soil conditions such as during droughts, like eggplants, asparagus, and okra; where other plants won't even begin to seed.

Therefore, to have a successful vegetable garden, you must first ensure the soil you have is healthy enough for your plants. Soil is critical in helping plants grow and giving us the nutrients we consume when eating them.

If the soil you are planting your vegetables in is not healthy enough, it may mean your harvest will not have the necessary nutrients you need in them. This means you will be consuming far fewer nutrients from them! Therefore, the soil affects the vegetable plants as well as your health.

FIVE TYPES OF SOIL

Silt Soil: This is one of the most fertile soil types as it is very nutrient-dense. It is usually very fluffy, and when watered, it has good water drainage and retains water well. Unfortunately, this soil can be compacted and hard, causing poor plant growth and damage to roots.

Clay Soil: It's alkaline, usually lumpy, dense, and heavier than other soils. Clay soil is the most challenging soil to work with as it tends to change seasonally, retains water well in cooler weather, and quickly dries up in hot weather. It too can get quite compacted during the hardening process, causing damage to plants or slowing plant growth.

However, due to its nature, it tends to be very nutrient-dense, with the right minerals to grow healthy vegetables. It retains water well and is best suited for growing vegetables that require lots of moisture or water.

Sandy Soil: It's less fertile, acidic, very rough, and light due to the larger soil particles it has. It does not retain water well, so it loses a lot of the minerals and nutrients your vegetable plants will need. Maintaining its fertility will require a lot of financial investment over time.

Chalk Soil: This has a very high concentration of calcium carbonate; it's very alkaline and tends to be quite lumpy and dense. Water drainage can be difficult to achieve with this soil.

Loam Soil: It's an ideal fertile soil that is great for most plants, and it has a lovely combination of clay, sandy, and silt soil. It's water drainage helps it retain moisture in hot and cold conditions without drowning plants with too much water. Due to its nature, it has minerals and retains them, making it a high-quality soil.

SIGNS OF HIGH-QUALITY AND FERTILE SOIL

Now we know the importance of good soil and the different soil types. You may have a few questions, and you may be curious to understand if your soil is healthy or not; what you could do to make it fertile enough to grow nutritious vegetables.

What Is Fertile Soil?

It's essentially one that can maintain the growth of vegetable plants. Its soil can give plants the necessary nutrients to grow and contain their natural nutrients for human consumption.

The soil conditions need to be good for the plant's roots to grow as much as they need and for the plant to get the necessary water; fertile soil will do both. The soil texture also affects fertility; therefore, fertile soil does not have rocks and weeds, which may prevent the healthy growth of plants.

This kind of soil is considered high-quality soil. It's what gardeners worldwide work hard to achieve and maintain for their gardens.

Fertile soil for vegetable gardening has the following characteristics:

- It has efficient internal water drainage.
- There's good moisture retention, although not drowning plants.
- It has essential minerals and nutrients.
- Its well-aerated soil allows air circulation and avoids the consequences of compaction.
- It's free of debris and pollution, such as stone and plastic.
- It's free from weeds and nutrient-stealing plants that prevent proper growth.
- It's free from infestations of worms or insects that pose a risk to the development of plants.
- It's rich in organic matter, such as compost or aged manure. Organic matter provides nutrients to

plants. When a garden is rich in these resources, the soil will provide nutrients for the plants to grow, which means artificial fertilizers are often unnecessary.

- It doesn't feel compacted and hard.
- It's not too sandy, as this makes the soil lose its nutrients.

STEPS TO PREPARE YOUR SOIL

Step 1: Test Your Soil

Take a handful of soil from your garden and place it into a plastic container to get it tested. There are different tests for different purposes, and some are very important. For instance, you will need to do a pH test, as some vegetables require a specific pH to grow, so it's essential to know your soil levels.

Not knowing if it's alkaline or acidic can prevent your vegetables from absorbing the nutrients in your soil and growing correctly. Typically a pH of around 6.5 is good enough to produce good results for most plants.

Depending on what you are testing for, you can find the test at a local garden store, or you may need to use a testing laboratory. Using a soil-testing laboratory with specialized knowledge and testing may seem daunting and expensive; however, it will reveal as much information as possible.

The professionals may also be able to diagnose your soil and give you a good report on what your soil needs.

Testing your soil is beneficial to your success, as it helps you avoid failure because it prevents financial waste on products that may be of no use or harmful to your plants.

A typical gardener with no knowledge starts planting without running tests; as a result, they are gambling and playing a guessing game. When you test your soil, you will know exactly what it needs, has, or where it can be improved.

You will then spend your money on the right treatments and avoid buying things aimlessly with no specific problem to solve.

Step 2: Clean Your Soil

Gather up your gardening tools! If you have a traditional in-ground garden, use a garden fork to loosen and soften the hard and compacted soil. To know if you have done a good job at loosening up the soil, is if it crumbles up and is soft when you hold it in your hand.

To help with this, you can wet the area you are working on to make softening and digging easier. It's advised to dig as deep as 10 inches. If you have already purchased containers or raised beds, this step may be left out.

Remove rocks, stones, weeds, or anything considered unwanted debris from your soil. Use a garden rake over the surface of your soil to ensure all debris is removed. This can be a lot of fun and tiring work, so take your time and rest in between should you need to.

Step 3: Remove Infestations

Bugs, worms, and weeds can damage your soil. Some infestations can do more harm to the vegetables themselves and not the soil. However, the harvest will also turn out bad if the soil is in bad condition.

To avoid disappointment, make sure before planting your vegetables that you don't have any infestations that may be of concern. If your soil has some insect infestation that poses a risk to your vegetable growth, you will need to get rid of the infestation before planting.

However, remember not to remove all kinds of insects; some can benefit your garden and are essential to your garden's natural ecosystem. Not everything is a potential threat! Insects such as bees, ladybugs, and ants are good to have, but some, like cabbage worms, mites, and carrot rust flies need to be kept out of your garden.

Step 4: Treat Your Soil

Once you know the state of your soil, it's important to follow up with what it needs and what's missing. You can use manure or compost to increase minerals in your soil, as this increases its fertility.

Follow the instructions on when to use the products, the frequency, and how to apply them. In some cases, especially when not using the in-ground garden option, you can buy soil already fertile for your containers or raised beds.

This allows you to avoid stressing about your soil quality. However, make sure the soil supplier you are using is trustworthy, and their soil is as good as they say it is. This is why it's imperative to learn about soil fertility and quality—whether you buy soil or cultivate it yourself.

STORE-BOUGHT VS. HOMEMADE SOIL TREATMENTS

There are various ways to treat your soil, from products you buy from a store or homemade ones. Depending on the kind of gardener you want to be, you may prefer buying products ready to use or getting your hands dirty by creating your own. Both options have their benefits, so you should consider them all carefully.

Homemade Soil Treatments

Some gardeners started their own home vegetable gardens because they wanted more control over what goes into their bodies. These gardeners are typically very conscious of ingredient lists and ensure that they do not consume chemicals—especially those that could be harmful to their health! If this is you, homemade soil treatments may offer you peace of mind from worrying about what goes into your food.

That's because modern-day soil treatments are made from non-organic ingredients or a mixture of organic and non-organic ingredients. As someone who wants your food to be whole, organic, and nutrient-dense, you might be reluctant to use these modern-day treatments.

You may want to have the most organic harvest possible and want to eliminate chemicals and synthetic minerals. There are some amazing benefits of choosing this route to treat your soil, but there are some disadvantages.

You will have to determine if this choice is worth any possible risks or downsides it will come with. You can create your homemade compost and manure, which will help you in the long run with the profitability of your vegetable garden.

Advantages

- You will save a lot of money and be able to make some treatments in bulk with already existing free ingredients.
- You will have a higher return on your investment.
- You can know the specific quantity of what you feed your vegetable crops, unlike store-bought treatments where you may speculate and hope you have enough of something.

Disadvantages

- The period it takes to make homemade treatments can be lengthy. It may be months before you finally use your compost and manure.
- You can't always be sure that your treatments give your vegetable plants exactly what they need. Extra testing for your homemade treatments may be necessary in some cases.
- It requires work on your part, such as constant maintenance and upkeep of the conditions of your treatments.

Store-Bought Soil Treatments

For fairly new gardeners modern-day and store-bought fertilizers may be more appealing than homemade ones.

Not all store-bought soil treatments are inadequate; in fact, many stores today sell prepackaged organic treatments.

However you may not be able to trust some brands as some are not "regulated," and organic can mean anything or something totally different to each person. However, the right store treatments can be efficient, effective and will produce results.

You don't have to feel guilty about not being "fully in control" of everything in your gardening process. Just like homemade soil treatments, store-bought treatments have their benefits and disadvantages. You will need to decide which works best for you.

Advantages

- It saves you lots of time, as you buy products when you need them and use them when you need them.
- You don't have to wait months for treatment to mature before you use it.

Disadvantages

- It requires you to be mindful of the brands you pick and learn as much as you can about ingredients. This will help you avoid bad and potentially harmful soil treatments.
- Compared to homemade treatments, store-bought ones can be more costly when maintaining your garden.

DECIDING WHAT TO GROW

To know which vegetables to grow, you will first need to understand "Why" you want to grow them in the first place. Is it because you want to supplement the food and vegetables in the house? Then you need to grow the vegetables you need or eat the most.

There are various reasons for starting our gardens—those reasons will help you decide what to grow. With this in mind, it's important to factor in the gardening space or type of garden you have.

For example, you might have a small gardening space but want to grow vegetables fit for a large family - this might be challenging for you to achieve. You might want a certain kind of vegetable not organically grown or available in your area, so growing this type of vegetable in your garden is a good idea.

You might need to get more salad into your diet - then, you will need to grow salad vegetables such as lettuce, herbs, tomatoes, and cucumbers. You might be concerned about the quality of the onions you buy from a local store, and is looking for better alternative.

Growing your onions will help you control their quality, as you are in charge of the garden's soil, watering, and general upkeep.

When deciding what to grow, you must also consider your soil type and pH levels. Not all vegetables can grow in all types of soil or pH levels—some vegetables need very acidic soil, and some need very alkaline soil.

If you attempt to grow a vegetable plant that needs an alkaline environment in an acidic environment, chances are it won't grow properly. This might cause your gardening efforts to be wasted, and you might feel like you're a failure when the problem is that the plant is in the wrong soil conditions.

Therefore, if you want a successful garden, you need to grow what will be most successful for your soil type.

You might need to change your diet due to health problems, and perhaps your doctor has asked you to eat specific vegetables that cannot grow well in your soil.

In this case, you will need to be careful with the type of garden you choose, as the soil that is the hardest to amend is the natural earth in your yard. This means you will need to choose a type of garden with soil you can control as much as possible.

In this scenario, raised beds or container gardens are preferred. Additionally, you can buy soil that's already the right kind for your desired vegetables.

If you want a vegetable supply that goes on and on for months without replanting again, you will need to grow vegetables that can easily and quickly regrow.

If you are concerned about not being full enough or want to grow more filling vegetables for you and your family, then growing starchy vegetables will be the best choice. If you want a garden that requires the least work, you will need to grow vegetables that require less pruning and upkeep.

If you want to save lots of water with your garden, you will need to focus your garden on vegetables that require the least amount of water to grow strong. You might lack a specific nutrient, such as vitamin A, and want alternatives to vitamin supplements. You can then grow vegetables high in vitamin A such as butternut squash and pumpkin.

SOWING AND PLANTING SEEDS: SOW FAR, SOW GOOD

Now that you have decided what you want to plant let's get into all you need to know about how to start. Planting and sowing may seem relatively straightforward; however, it can go horribly wrong if not fully understood.

This is because the depth of a seed or plant in the soil influences how it grows. For example, some seeds need to be planted around an inch in the soil. If these plants are planted far deeper than an inch, they can take longer to show their growth on the soil's surface.

Therefore, it's important to first understand the kind of vegetables you want to plant and how best to plant them. Each vegetable plant may require a different planting method.

Some vegetable plants are fragile and may need to be grown in a container garden pot and planted in the ground once they have become seedlings.

Therefore, the method you use to plant the vegetables you want is crucial to the success of your garden. Below are some insightful and effective sowing techniques for planting.

Some may be useful in the type of garden you want, and some may not, but it's always good to know various techniques. You never know when you might want to change things up and grow something different or expand your garden to accommodate more vegetables.

SOWING TECHNIQUES

Broadcasting

This method of sowing or planting is mainly for traditional outdoor gardens. It's relaxed and less "scientific" because the seeds are randomly scattered around on the ground.

Seeds may or may not be covered with soil. This method is done either by hand or with the help of a tractor to mechanically scatter the seeds all over the soil.

Advantages

- It's one of the quickest methods.
- It's the cheapest method to sow seeds, especially for a large area when you don't have enough time or money to invest in other sowing methods.
- It can be used for container or raised bed gardens, as well.

Disadvantages

- It causes seed overcrowding.
- It's only suitable for seeds that don't need a specific amount of space to grow.
- It's only suitable for shallow-rooted plants.

Dibbling

With this method of sowing, you will make holes in the ground, container, or raised bed soil to put the seeds inside and cover them with soil.

The holes typically accommodate either seeds, seedlings, or bulbs. This will depend on your type of garden and the type of vegetable plants you want to grow. This method is typically more "scientific" because a specific amount of space needs to be kept between plants.

Advantages

- It can be done in all types of gardens.
- It can create enough necessary space for what you need to grow.
- It's very organized and accurate.

Disadvantages

- It's a very time-consuming process.
- It requires more effort to make sure there is specific amount of space between each hole/plants.

Drilling

This method uses a tractor-drilling machine or handheld drill to drill a hole in the ground. The machine drills in seeds and instantly closes or covers the hole with soil.

The soil it's drilled in or which covers it is usually compacted. It drills seeds into the ground in a straight line, creating enough space for seeds.

Advantages

- Fast and methodical.
- Seeds are covered right after being drilled in.
- No need to go back and cover the seeds or make sure they are inserted properly.
- There are cheaper alternatives to tractor drillers that are effective.
- You can roughly calculate how many seeds are needed based on the area you'll be working on.
- You will likely need fewer seeds to sow.
- You can drill in other important things, such as nutrients and minerals from fertilizers or manures at the same time.

Disadvantages

- It can be expensive to do and buy the equipment.
- It can be time-consuming, especially when using a handheld drill.

Plough Sowing

This form of sowing is one of the oldest and most traditional methods. It typically relies on a person's labor to be efficient and effective in sowing seeds.

The plow can be pulled by cattle or a tractor, and as the plow digs into the ground, seeds are thrown into the rows the plow makes. Traditionally seeds are thrown in right after the rows are made or continuously with the plow as the rows are being dug.

When using a plow machine, the machine itself will be set in a way that allows it to immediately throw seeds into each row it digs.

Advantages

- It can be less costly when cattle are used.
- It's a fast way to sow seeds.
- It's great for large, traditional in-ground gardens.

Disadvantages

- It can be expensive, especially with plow machines.
- Seeds can become overcrowded.

Planting

This method is one that typically uses already germinated seeds, plants, bulbs, and seedlings to be planted in the ground for them to grow.

Advantages

- It allows you to be intentional in protecting fragile vegetable plants.
- It can be a quick process if you buy already germinated plants to grow.

Disadvantages

- It takes time to start planting if you are germinating the plants yourself.

- It's also time-consuming, as you would need to be very careful.

Transplanting

This method of sowing is also called "replanting," which is taking out a plant from where it has been planted, moving it to another area or garden, and planting it there. This can be done across most gardens depending on the type of plant being replanted.

Advantages

- It's a quick movement of plants.
- Transplanting makes it easy and possible to move plants across locations.
- You can rehabilitate plants and soil.

Disadvantages

- There's a chance of roots being damaged when done wrong.
- Not all plants may survive.
- A different soil may hurt or damage the plant when replanting.

READY, SET, GROW!

Now that you know how to sow your seeds, you have officially started your exciting gardening journey. Wait and pay close attention to your garden.

Patience and staying consistent with the right watering and maintenance schedule are extremely important. It's important to take note of the growth timeline of your garden and know exactly what to expect.

Each vegetable plant will differ in how they grow, how fast they mature, and such. This growing time will expose problems with the soil, plants, and any issues you need to fix.

It's also a great time to use compost in your soil or other treatments to encourage proper growth or prevent bugs and other infestations which could destroy your garden. Your garden may or may not need to be covered to protect it from outside harm, so monitoring it is essential.

Pay attention to how the soil retains and drains the water, remove any weeds or rocks, and fix compacted soil. If your vegetable plants are not receiving enough sun and suffering in the area they are in, you might need to move them.

This is easy when you have a container garden - however, moving plants in a traditional in-ground or raised bed garden may be challenging. This may call for replanting and taking plants out to put them in a better environment where they will get enough sun.

However if your planning stages were thorough prior to planting your seeds, you'll have nothing to worry about.

CHAPTER 2
GROWING YOUR SALAD TOMATOES

Tomatoes are one of the most popular vegetables to grow in home gardens. They are relatively easy to care for, and they produce an abundance of flavorful fruit.

Homegrown tomatoes often taste better than store-bought varieties, and they can provide a nutritious addition to your diet. In addition, growing your own tomatoes can save you money and provide you with a sense of satisfaction.

There is nothing quite like harvesting your own homegrown tomatoes and using them in your favorite recipes. If you are thinking about starting a garden, tomatoes are a great option.

With a little care and attention, you can enjoy delicious tomatoes all summer long.

THE RIGHT SOIL FOR TOMATOES

Tomatoes can do well being planted in most soil types if the soil has good drainage and is healthy or fertile enough. Therefore, tomato plants are typically not problematic and not too difficult to grow.

You may not have to buy soil or make any drastic changes unless your soil is dangerously unhealthy. Purchase some manure and other necessary treatments to make sure your soil is in the right condition for your tomato plants to grow.

Remember to use soil testing kits before purchasing any treatments to avoid wasting money. First, know exactly what your soil condition is, and then proceed with what exactly is needed for your soil.

Tomatoes love soil with enough organic material; therefore, ensure your soil has enough of the material to begin with. Tomatoes prefer a bit more acidic soil conditions to grow healthy and strong. So ensure your pH levels are between 5.8 and 6.8.

Tomato Plant Diseases

When planting any plant, especially vegetables, it's important to do all you can to avoid the possibility of the roots of your plant rotting and dying. With tomato plants, there are some causes of root disease.

These can be planting your tomatoes in soil previously used to grow other plants such as potatoes, eggplants, and even tomatoes. If your soil was used for such plants recently, you will need to wait at least two years before planting your tomatoes in the same soil.

Although this might sound shocking and drastic, root disease is a risk, and it can kill off your tomato plants which you have worked so hard to grow and prepare for.

Some may find success in growing their tomato plants in soil that grew other vegetables, but the result is not always successful: It's a gamble. However, you can plant tomatoes close to other vegetable plants such as carrots, garlic, and onions.

Avoid planting close to the vegetables below:

- Cabbage
- Kale
- Corn
- Horseradish
- Potatoes
- Broccoli
- Turnip
- Rutabaga
- Arugula
- Cress
- Radish
- Mustard
- Kohlrabi
- Cauliflower
- Fennel

When your tomato plants have root disease, they will change color—some will turn yellow, wilt, and die. You might try lots of things to revive them, such as watering them more in the hopes this will help, but unfortunately it wont help.

You might be overwatering them and causing more damage. Root rot and disease can be caused by fungal and bacterial infections, which may spread once one plant is infected.

This means removing any suspected infected tomato plants as soon as possible is important to prevent further damage to others. Unfortunately, treating the already infected plants may be challenging, so it's always best to plant a new seedling instead.

However, avoid planting the new seedlings in the same soil as the infected plants, as they will get infected and could potentially die. Therefore, plant new seedlings in new clean and fertile soil, free of bacteria or fungi.

After removing the infected plant(s), it's important to disinfect all the tools you used to touch them and the soil, as not doing so will transfer the infection onto other tomato plants.

You can use alcohol disinfectants and boiling water to clean the tools or equipment. Only after this process can you use them again on other healthy plants.

HOW TO SOW TOMATOES

Correct Season to Plant Tomatoes

Tomatoes typically grow best in the warmer seasons—this can be in spring or early summer, which is anywhere from late May to August. They also need quite a lot of sunlight, and it's best to keep them in a space where they are fully exposed to sunlight. Tomatoes will need around six hours of direct sunlight for proper growth.

Planting Needs and Requirements

Tomato plants are best planted after they have already germinated from a seed in a container with no soil but organic matter. Therefore, the best method for growing tomatoes is not placing the seed directly in the soil but first germinating it in a separate location or container.

Once you have your tomato seeds in hand, you can use a plant container with good drainage to insert your organic matter without soil and place your seeds inside. The number of seeds per container will depend on how large the plant container is.

Each seed must be inserted about half an inch deep into the organic matter. If you are unclear about what matter to use for the seeds, you can buy and use a good seed starting mix at a trusted store. This will ensure you avoid mistakes along the way with growing seedlings.

You can use containers around the house, and you don't have to buy special seedling containers. Depending on your gardening space, if you want to have a large tomato garden, it may be useful to get a special seedling container to separate all your seeds and be able to germinate as many as possible.

By germinating the seed first, you want to get it to "sprout" and then transplant the seedling to its final and permanent location. The temperature is incredibly important in this germinating phase. Since tomatoes love warmer conditions, you must ensure they are warm enough at around 70 to 80 °F.

Cold temperatures can easily stall their growth! Once your seeds are placed in the containers, you will need to lightly water them. You can use a light spray to ensure the seeds or seedlings are not drowning in water.

You should start to see the seeds germinate in a week. Once you can see the seedlings, you must place the containers directly under sunlight for around at last six hours a day. You do not need to germinate the tomato seeds outside under direct sunlight, as most seed germination is done indoors.

One of the reasons for this is to control the temperature the seeds are exposed to, making sure they are warm enough, especially if you start germinating your seeds toward late May or spring when it's still a bit chilly outside. Your seedlings will be ready when at least four leaves have sprouted.

Spacing and Measurements

Once you have your seedlings, it's time to transplant them! You must ensure that the soil has moisture but is not drowning in water and has drained enough.

Now that your soil is ready, you will remove your seedlings from their containers with the matter they are growing in. Be careful not to hurt the seedlings or their roots during this stage, as any damage can delay growth or prevent the tomato plant from growing in the soil.

Now you will need to make holes in your soil of about half an inch or deeper depending on your seedling. Tomato seedlings will likely need to be deeper in the soil than in the organic matter.

When inserting your seedling, ensure that the lower parts of the stem with the first leaf or two are covered with soil to help it grow much stronger roots.

When spacing your tomato plants, there are a few things to consider. First if your tomato plants are determinate or indeterminate—this means if their growth, height, and width have any limits or not.

Depending on the type of tomatoes you are planting, some can grow very large and tall, so you need to space them farther apart to accommodate their growth. Some other tomato varieties do not grow too large or tall, so you can space them not too far apart, expecting they will not over-crowd each other.

Below is a spacing guide for tomato plant types that are determinate and indeterminate:

Determinate Tomato Varieties: These can be spaced 12–24 inches apart; they are the least to cause overcrowding and will likely not need staking or support.

Staked Indeterminate Tomato Varieties: These can be spaced 14–20 inches apart from each other and likely need help and support to control the nature of their "limitless growth."

They can typically be spaced as short as determinate varieties or shorter because of the support or staking they have. The staking directs their growth upward or in the desired direction to create enough space between plants.

Un-Staked Indeterminate Tomato Varieties: These can be spaced at around 24–36 inches apart; just like the above, they grow larger and need support. However, this kind is unsupported without staking, so they need a much larger space in between to avoid crowding.

WATERING TOMATOES

You should water your tomato plants as often as necessary. Since the warmer tomato planting seasons are hot, it is advisable to water your plants every two or three days.

You may want a specific guide on how much you should water your tomato plants; however, the frequency is determined by a couple factors, such as temperature and the kind of soil you have. As a gardener, you must be in tune with your garden and go through a phase of figuring it out.

That means studying how well it absorbs water, how quickly it stays moist, how your plants respond to your regular watering schedule, and how different temperatures affect your soil and your tomato plants' watering needs.

All of this will help you determine a more solid and accurate idea as to how often your plants need watering. However, there will be days when it rains, for example, and days like this will change your watering schedule; in the same way, other factors will also affect your watering schedule.

Always alter or adjust your watering schedule during the rainy season to prevent overwatering your tomato plants. You can determine if your tomatoes need more or less water by inspecting their soil, looking at it, and feeling it.

Sometimes, you might need to dig in the soil to inspect its moisture. It needs to be moist and not drenched or saturated in water. Preventing water saturation can also help you avoid root rot disease.

How To Water Tomatoes

To prevent overwatering, it's important to water your tomato plants slowly, meaning the pressure of your water should not be harsh, and the amount of water used should be gradual.

This allows the water to properly reach the deeper levels of the soil and drench it well. Gradual watering will also help you avoid giving your garden too much water because as you water your garden, you can easily see how your soil responds.

Too much water at once does not give you enough time to determine if it is enough or if you have gone overboard. Water your tomato plants from the root instead of watering the plant down. This will help you protect your tomato plants from developing any infections and attracting harmful insects.

You may also find mulch very useful in ensuring that your plants are protected from quick water evaporation and dryness in the soil. Mulch can be bought and poured on the surface of your soil and around your tomato plants. This also creates some insulation and keeps moisture in longer.

FERTILIZATION FOR TOMATOES

Tomatoes need fertilization when planted in the soil, as they need and consume quite a lot of minerals and nutrients. They grow healthier, stronger, and quicker when they are fertilized.

You can use either organic or chemical fertilizers for your tomato garden—make sure to pick the high-quality fertilizer that will give you the best results.

However, remember that fertilization will always depend on your soil's current state and condition. Therefore, knowing your soil first is very important.

How Often Do Tomatoes Need Fertilization?

Typically, tomato plants need fertilization when first planted in the garden soil. It is always best to wait until the plants start to grow to fertilize the soil again or until the plants start growing tomatoes.

You can then fertilize every month or every six weeks, depending on your garden's needs. The fertilizer you choose needs a good balance between nitrogen, phosphorus, and potassium.

The balance should be as equal as possible or one where phosphorus is higher than the other two. Too much nitrogen should be avoided, and a good balance is best, as a nitrogen overdose can cause your tomatoes to grow big stems and huge leaves but no fruit or actual tomatoes. This is why testing your soil first is important.

TOMATO GROWING STAGES

The end game of planting tomato plants is to get juicy, red, and yummy tomatoes to eat in delicious meals. How long will it take to get to this stage? It can take anywhere from 45 to 70 days for your tomato plants to start producing tomatoes. The harvesting period can be anywhere from 21 to 145 days.

PROTECTING YOUR TOMATOES

Tomato plants can be a target to many hungry worms, insects, and birds. It can be heartbreaking to one day walk up to your beautiful garden and discover that your red, juicy tomatoes have been eaten by something, and now they are wasted! There are some ways you can protect your tomato plants and prevent these heartbreaking possibilities.

Cold Temperatures

Unfortunately, tomato plants despise the cold and don't grow well in cold conditions. It's also unfortunate that some days during the warmer seasons, cold fronts happen, and on some nights or days, it can get a bit chilly for your plants.

You can prevent damage to your tomato garden by covering your plants with a type of cover that keeps your plants warm and still gives them enough room to grow.

Protect Tomatoes From Animals and Insects

If your tomato garden is left vulnerable, pets, chickens, squirrels, and other animals can cause damage to it. It can save you a lot of stress and tears by creating a barrier that will keep your plants safe, such as a cage or barrier that is hard to unlock, break, or move.

It's also a good idea to get a cage that makes it difficult for the plants to get damaged through the holes. If using a cage is not an option, you can always use raised beds or containers you can move to a safer location.

Raised beds can be made in a way that makes it difficult for most domestic animals to easily access the plants. You can further protect your garden from birds by covering it with material that prevents them from eating or picking at the plants or tomatoes.

An elevated garden or one not in the ground can be one smart way to fight very common insects and worms that plague the traditional kind of garden. However, should you have an in-ground garden, using frames and stakes to support your tomato plants and elevating them off the ground can help minimize insect damage.

You can further prevent cutworms or other types of worms from damaging your plants by using a cone or cylinder around your plants. This will make it harder for the worms to access your tomatoes.

Another preventive measure you can take is to clean your garden as much as needed to remove dead leaves, dirt, or anything that could attract these pest. If these methods don't work, go to your local store to buy a non-toxic solution that can clear your garden of snails, worms, and insects and other pests.

MAINTAINING YOUR TOMATO GARDEN

Pruning Tomato Plants

Prune your tomato plants, as this will help them grow more and grow properly. It also prevents crowding between your plants which can lessen the growth needed.

Because disease and pest infestation are more likely when plants are overcrowded, trimming is an excellent way to keep your tomato crop healthy. Pruning is especially important for indeterminate tomato varieties, as they will likely cause the most problems with their rapid and constant growth.

When pruning, remove or shave off suckers from the bottom of the stem, and each time these suckers show up, trim them off. Don't trim too much or too hard, as this may cause the plant to produce more suckers.

Support the Structural Growth

Prevent growth stagnation and disease by supporting your plants and getting them off the ground as much as possible. Use sticks or supporting structures to hold them in place and to grow upright as much as possible.

HARVESTING TOMATOES

Now, to the fun part: harvesting! This is the most exciting part of planting vegetables—being able to pick them and enjoy them. Depending on the kind of tomato you have planted, you will know when your tomatoes are ready to be harvested and picked when the color has changed to red—sometimes a pinky red.

The stems holding the tomatoes may also change to a more yellow color and seem weaker. You can also feel the tomato, and when it's firm but has a slight softness to them, you will know they are ready. The smell is also one of the ways you can tell if they are ready—when it changes from a raw scent to a sweeter, tomato-like scent.

SAVING TOMATO SEEDS

You can save the seeds from your harvested tomatoes by simply scooping them out of the tomatoes. You will then put the scooped-out seeds onto a dry paper towel for them to dry.

Once the seeds are dry, you will store them in a clean container with zero moisture. When you are ready to sow tomatoes again, you can use your dried and harvested seeds!

CHAPTER 3
GROWING YOUR SALAD CUCUMBERS

G rowing cucumbers is a rewarding experience that can provide you with an abundance of fresh, crisp vegetables. They are also highly versatile, and can be used in salads, sandwiches, and even as a refreshing beverage. When you grow your own cucumbers, you can be sure that they are free of chemicals and other pollutants.

There's nothing like slicing into a crisp cucumber that you've grown yourself. Plus, homegrown cucumbers are incredibly easy to grow. All you need is a sunny spot in your garden and some basic gardening supplies, so let's get right into it.

THE RIGHT SOIL FOR CUCUMBERS

Cucumbers grow best in a specific soil type, such as sandy loose soil. However, they can grow in other types of soil as long as the soil used is well-drained and fertile enough.

Cucumbers prefer soil with enough organic material; therefore, ensure your soil has enough of it.

Cucumbers do well in a slightly acidic soil environment with pH levels between 5.5 and 7. These plants grow really deep roots—so this is something to consider when choosing your type of garden. If you want a container or raised bed garden, ensure the plants have enough space to grow their roots deep. Their roots can be around three to four feet deep.

Cucumber Plant Diseases

Cucumber plants have some risk of getting root disease which can be caused by fungi and bacteria. The root of the cucumber plant can become infected and spread to other areas causing the plant to die in a much different fashion than the tomato plant.

One of the simplest ways to prevent root rot and disease is to avoid planting cucumbers with plants like tomatoes in the same area you have planted in the past two years.

This means finding an alternative in-ground area to plant that is fertile or using containers and raised beds to grow your cucumbers.

Since cucumbers can be prone to infections and disease, it's always a good choice to grow the strongest kind and one resistant to the typical challenges most varieties face. This will make it easy for you and help you enjoy gardening without the constant fear of losing your entire crop.

Also avoid planting the below near your cucumber garden or in the same soil as them:

- Potatoes
- Melons
- Sage

Cucumber plants show very similar signs of root disease as other plants; however, the leaves do not always change color to yellow as a sign. Instead, the cucumber leaves all wilt on an infected plant; they wilt rapidly and typically at once.

Therefore, you will need to look out for any wilting leaves to determine if your garden may have a possible infection you need to fix.

Some infections can be treated with soil fumigation or steam fertilization; however, depending on how well the solutions fixes the problem, you could continue to grow your cucumbers and harvest them.

Unfortunately, the infection means not being able to replant in that same soil for some time. It's also advised to not touch other plants or cucumber plants with the same tools and equipment you used for the infected ones. Prevent the spread of infection with an alcohol disinfectant and use hot water to wash tools.

HOW TO SOW CUCUMBERS

Correct Season To Plant Cucumbers

Cucumbers need to be planted in warm temperatures from late May until August to get the best results and growth. Much like tomatoes, they only prefer warmth, and sunlight is incredibly important.

They must be under direct sunlight for as much as possible for most of the day. If they do not have enough sun exposure, they will likely not produce fruit; if they do, the fruit will be of bad quality.

Like tomatoes, cucumbers need at least six hours of sunlight exposure daily. Therefore, ensure they are planted in a good location or area. The correct temperatures they need are between 65 and 75 °F.

Planting Needs And Requirements

It's best to first germinate cucumber seeds indoors before planting them in the soil outside. The plants during the germination period can be susceptible to cold temperatures, which can stall their growth. Therefore, make sure that the temperature of the soil is around 60 to 85 °F and not lower.

The air temperature must also be around 75 °F for the best conditions to begin germination. To germinate cucumber seeds, you will need to use containers of your choice and ensure they can drain water well.

You will need to use a seed-starting mixture and pour it into your containers—these typically have no soil. You will then need to sow seeds in a one-inch deep hole, cover it, and lightly spray it with water. It's best to put one seed per pot, but you can put two in case the other dies or is not strong enough.

The seedlings will start to sprout in a week or around ten days, and during this time, you will then remove seedlings that appear weak from the pots—that's if you use the strategy of planting two in one pot.

Cucumber plants can grow quite high and be very unruly; you will need to control the plant's growth by supporting its structure. Holding up the stems and letting the cucumber grow by hanging them down is one of the effective methods of growing them.

There are two types of cucumber plants: the bushy kind and the vine kind. The bushy kind is best grown in a container, and the vine is best grown in the ground.

Spacing And Measurements

Once you have seedlings, you can then prepare to transplant them into the garden of your choice. Make sure you lightly water or soak your seedlings if you want a more rapid germination phase once they're replanted.

Soaking can help the process move faster in some cases. To avoid challenges with removing seedlings from their containers or trays, it might be helpful to use biodegradable containers.

This will make the transplanting process easier on you and the seedlings because you will avoid damaging them. Depending on your seedlings, you will plant vine types of cucumbers as deep as 12–14 inches deep in the soil.

The bushy cucumber types can be planted as deep as 12–16 inches. Cucumber plants should further be spaced 36–60 inches apart from each other.

MAINTAINING YOUR CUCUMBER GARDEN

Cucumbers need special care and attention; however, they are not difficult to grow and maintain. By following the below steps, you will surely and successfully grow them into a beautiful harvest.

Pruning Your Cucumbers

If you want your cucumber plant to grow well and produce healthy fruit, you must control how it grows. You will do this by trimming or removing parts of it that are damaged or leaves that may prevent your plant from getting enough sunlight.

Cucumbers can grow into unruly plants, making it hard to keep track of their growth and ensure that their fruit is healthy. Pruning is a necessary step in maintaining your plant's health and longevity.

It also allows you to pick up any issues, such as infestations or diseases in the plant. What should you trim? You can cut down unhealthy branches and any leaves or branches that grow right at the bottom of the stem—also known as suckers, which we mentioned earlier with tomatoes.

When you prune your cucumber plant, you must cut it as close to the stem as possible; this avoids uneven growth.

Watering Cucumbers

Cucumber plants thrive in moist soil, so keep it moist by watering it regularly. Your plants will need roughly one to two inches of water each week.

You could get away with watering your plants once or twice a week. Cucumbers can be quite easy to grow, especially when you follow the simple steps in this book. You can enjoy watering them with a hose from a chair to rest and protect your back while enjoying being out in nature.

Once you are done watering your cucumber garden, you can pour mulch on the soil's surface like you would with tomatoes. This is so the moisture and warmth remain in the soil for as long as possible, as well as to prevent pests.

Only water your cucumbers when the soil needs more water; otherwise, avoid watering. When the soil on the surface and right beneath is dry but far deeper in is moist, it's time to water the soil again. Remember to constantly monitor your soil, as all soil types drain water differently, which might affect its water retention.

However, once you have a good idea of the kind of soil you have, you will be able to determine when to water your cucumbers and how much.

Fertilization For Cucumbers

Cucumbers may be grown without fertilizer, but the fruit might not be the best or grow far too small. This happens with most vegetable plants, so supporting your cucumber garden's growth with additional fertilization, nutrients, and minerals is important.

If you want the most nutritious harvest, you should fertilize the soil when you transplant them roughly twice a month and when you are covering the soil surface with mulch.

Avoid buying fertilizers with extremely high nitrogen levels, as it will cause your cucumbers to grow leaves and stems, not the actual cucumber. Use good quality fertilizer for your soil. This can be in the form of compost or manure; some of the best have been aged for a good period.

Unlike excessive chemical nitrogen fertilizers, compost won't harm your cucumber plants; where the nutrients will remain in your soil for longer.

PROTECTING YOUR CUCUMBERS

The first and most important step in protecting your cucumber plants is to plant them in the right season to avoid cold weather damage. Also, plant them in the right soil and environmental conditions to avoid disease and pests.

Cold Temperatures

To protect your cucumbers from frost and cold damage, you will need to cover the plants or plant them in a space that serves as a shelter. A sheltered space will lessen the cold damage, as winds affect your garden less.

Try to consistently monitor weather changes, for example checking weather conditions and climates in advance — this will help you foresee any possible cold damage. If you know that one particular day or night might be very cold, you can protect your garden by covering it on those days.

You don't need to buy anything special to cover your plants; you can use any light yet protective covering such as newspapers, plastic, or a large cotton cloth.

Secure the coverage on the sides to ensure that it stays in place all day and night until you need to remove it. You can hold up the covering with sticks, a nearby fence or use rocks to hold it down instead.

Another useful method is to create a barrier around your plants to protect them from the incoming cold winds. You don't need anything special; you can use anything that can shield your plants and create a cone effect around them.

Protect Cucumbers From Pests

Protecting your cucumbers from pests is not just to prevent them from being eaten but to avoid any infections the pests may bring along. Some infections can be trans-mitted from the pest or insect to the plant itself and cause it to die or infect other plants around it.

Pests that can do this to a cucumber in a garden are known as "cucumber beetles." They are very problematic, as they can infect the cucumbers with bacteria which makes the cucumber plants very sick, wilt, and die.

Other pests to watch out for are leaf miners, spider mites, whiteflies, and snails. We're sure you are curious about how to avoid these tiny damaging insects. You will need to make sure that you make cleaning your garden a habit.

Allowing your garden to have debris, weeds, and fallen leaves from other plants can attract garden pests like cucumber beetles. This also means ensuring that your soil is clean while you are waiting to plant vegetables such as cucumbers.

As a whole to prevent pests from damaging your plants, it is important to keep them out of your garden. You can do this by covering plants with fine mesh netting or row covers. Monitoring your plant consistently is just as important because you would want to catch any sign for infestations as soon as possible.

HARVESTING CUCUMBERS

The time you plant your seeds until you harvest your cucumbers will take approximately 30 and 70 days. This is exciting because you won't need to wait too long for harvest compared to other vegetable plants.

We're sure you'll probably be monitoring your cucumbers daily to see how big they get, and it can make you anxious to pick some already. This might further make you wonder when the right time to harvest them is and how you will know they are ready.

When cucumbers are harvested too early, they can have a distinct taste and texture that will make it hard for you to use them. In this case, it may be wise to pickle them, yet even in those cases, it may turn out bad.

However, many gardeners do love harvesting cucumbers that are not yet ripe. You might want to do this to avoid your cucumbers producing too many seeds or if you don't like succulent ones.

You will know your cucumbers are ready to be harvested when they are big enough—the expected size for the type of cucumber you are growing.

As cucumbers grow quite quickly, you can expect to harvest cucumbers every other day during its harvesting season. You can influence your plants to produce more cucumbers by pruning the vines and harvesting cucumbers.

The more cucumbers you harvest, the more vines will produce! That's because harvesting stimulates the vines to produce fruit in the same way pruning stimulates a plant to grow more. You can use garden scissors or a knife to cut off your ready cucumbers. Just make sure you cut them off clean to allow the vine to grow more.

Harvesting your cucumber fruit early in the day or morning is best. Cucumbers are typically sweeter and crisper than those that are picked later in the day.

The reason for this is that cucumbers contain a high amount of water, and as the day goes on, they tend to lose some of their water content through evaporation.

This not only affects the cucumber's flavor, but it can also reduce its shelf life. If a cucumber fruit appears to be small, not firm, or not a bright green color, this is a sign it is not ready. Cucumbers that are right for harvesting can range between two to eight inches in length.

If your goal is to ensure you have as many cucumbers as possible, you will need to take advantage of the warmer season by planting new cucumber plants every two to three weeks. This will allow you to harvest throughout the cucumber planting season and enjoy delicious cucumbers in your meals.

SAVING CUCUMBER SEEDS

Now that you have your harvest, you may already be planning your next planting season. You might wonder if you could avoid using store-bought seeds and instead use the ones from your harvest.

You can do this with cucumbers by scraping out their seeds; it's best to do this with a spoon and nothing too sharp to avoid damaging the seeds. The seeds will look soft and feel mushy, but that's normal.

Unfortunately, this is not advised if you want to plant them immediately, as the seeds may rot in the soil. You can place the seeds you've scraped out in a glass container or jar for a maximum of four days at room temperature. Stir the jar daily, making sure that you mix everything gently.

Each day, the seeds will start forming some fungus—do not be alarmed, as this is normal. The softshell of jelly that covers the seeds will start to drop down to the bottom of the jar and leave the seeds to float up.

You can then use water to rinse and separate the jelly from the seeds. Once the seeds are in hand, you will need to air-dry them. Spread the seeds on a plate or wooden tray and leave them out in cool, hot, and sunny weather conditions.

This will dry out the seeds enough for you to store them for use later or immediately after they are dry. To grow your cucumber plants from the dried seeds, you must follow the seed germination process again.

CHAPTER 4
GROWING YOUR
SALAD CABBAGES

Growing your own cabbages can be a fun and rewarding experience. For one, you'll get to enjoy the satisfaction of watching your cabbages grow from tiny seedlings to full-sized plants.

Plus, you'll be able to choose from a wide variety of cabbage varieties, including traditional green cabbages, red cabbages, and even savoy cabbages. And of course, there's nothing quite like the taste of freshly-picked cabbage straight from the garden.

But in addition to being delicious, cabbages are also packed with nutrients. They're an excellent source of Vitamins C and K, as well as fiber and antioxidants. So not only are they good for you, but they're good for the earth as well.

All in all, there are plenty of good reasons to grow your own cabbages and we will show you how to.

THE RIGHT SOIL FOR CABBAGES

Cabbages must be planted in firm soil to ensure their roots are secure and grow well without exposure. However, most soil will work fine provided it's fertile and with enough organic matter to provide the right growing conditions.

Like any vegetable plant, the soil needs good drainage. Most cabbages grow well in gardens with pH levels between 6 and 7.5. This pH level is especially important in curbing some plant diseases.

Cabbages love moisture and enough water, so the soil needs to hold moisture long enough, but it can also drain water to prevent root rotting and other plant diseases.

Cabbage Plant Diseases

Like any other vegetable plant, cabbage requires constant monitoring to detect illnesses, viruses, bacteria, and fungi that can slow or kill it.

Nothing is more frustrating than having everything in order, transplanting your seedlings into their forever home soil, and your plants dying a few weeks later. This can be disheartening; however, it's avoidable with the right care and efforts.

The possible diseases to look out for are Alternaria leaf spot, black rot, bottom rot, and clubroot disease. When preparing your soil for all your cabbage plants, you may need to avoid planting in the same soil that housed other plants such as potatoes, onions, and corn.

However, cabbage can grow well in soil that has grown peas and beans, as the soil following harvesting them is rich in nitrogen.

Cabbage plants need enough nitrogen to grow healthy and strong, as they are heavy fertilizer feeders and love nitrogen. Also avoid planting cabbages with or near strawberries, tomatoes, and grapes.

When the leaves turn black, yellow, or a funny yet distinct color, you can tell something is wrong with your cabbage plants. Sometimes, a disease might cause the leaves to turn yellow; however, in other cases, this may also be caused by overwatering your cabbage plants.

One of the simple ways to prevent some of the above-mentioned plant diseases is to ensure your soil has a pH above 7. Mosaic virus is a common kind of virus that infects all kinds of cabbages you may come across.

It has no cure and can be challenging to treat once it infects your garden. It's typically spread by weeds in the surrounding areas, which is why it's always a good thing to take time to clean out your garden as much as needed.

It may be hard to spot the infection, especially in the early stages, but you will be able to notice it at the base of a cabbage plant. You might see some dead spots with a change in color along the veins of the cabbage plant.

There might not be a cure for it, but you can surely take steps to prevent it, such as clearing out all weeds and debris regularly. This is true with most cabbage plant diseases—prevention is mostly through care and maintenance of your garden.

HOW TO SOW CABBAGES

Correct Season To Plant Cabbages

Cabbage plants can grow at different times in all four seasons. This is good news, as it means you can harvest cabbages throughout the year with careful planning and planting.

Cabbage plants are sensitive to harsh, cold temperatures like most plants, yet they can tolerate some cold weather—especially the varieties mainly grown in winter.

To ensure you have the right cabbage seeds for the season you are entering or are in, visit your local seed store. They will have a variety of cabbage seeds fit for each season.

Planting Needs And Requirements

Cabbages grow best when they are first germinated from seeds indoors. You will need to use small seedling containers for your seeds. If you want to plant cabbages in containers, you can plant one cabbage seed per container and have multiple containers of as many cabbages seeds as you like.

Make sure you use organic matter that is rich in minerals and nutrients instead of soil. It's always advised that you put more than one seedling in each container to offset any possible loss that may occur or infections of a seed.

That way, you don't waste your time; instead, you will replant another seedling that has already germinated from the same container. You can put roughly two to three seeds in one seedling container.

Place the seeds inside at around an inch or half an inch deep and water them by spraying water to moisten the organic matter enough to reach the soil. Just make sure not to oversaturate them. You will then let the seeds grow and germinate for about a month to six weeks.

Since you have put more than one seed in each container, you need to watch for the best-growing seedlings in each. You will then separate that particular seedling in its container to grow some healthy leaves.

Once the seedlings have produced strong and adult-like leaves, you will know they are ready to be transplanted into the ground or the garden of your choice.

At all times, ensure that your seedlings' organic matter is at roughly 75 °F for optimal growth.

Spacing And Measurements

Cabbage plants typically need to be planted in the ground, not in containers or raised bed gardens. However, growing cabbage in a container or raised bed is possible—you might be limited to how many you can grow, but it can work.

The kind of planting method best used for cabbages is in rows and wide enough from each other. With ready, prepared, and fertile soil, you will take your seedlings and put each in a row, leaving a space of about 18 inches between them.

This is so that each cabbage can have enough space to grow properly. Some varieties of cabbage may not need that much space, as they all vary in size.

However, 18 inches apart should accommodate all. When transplanting seedlings, make sure you plant them right at the end of the previous season before the correct one they are meant to be planted in.

That means if the type of cabbage you are planting best grows in summer, you will need to transplant them toward the end of spring. When planting your seedlings, be sure that your garden will have full sun exposure, as cabbages need at least six hours a day of sun exposure.

MAINTAINING YOUR CABBAGE GARDEN

Growing cabbages can be fairly easy to maintain once you know what to do and how. That is because cabbage plants are not too needy and problematic, provided that you take care of them as you should. Below, we will share with you some unique ways a cabbage garden needs care and love to be successful.

Pruning Your Cabbages

Make sure you always look out for any yellow or dying leaves and cut them off the cabbage plant. Trim parts that are damaged and not healthy. It can be easy for your cabbage plants to overgrow and fill the space around them or in between nearby cabbages.

This can make it hard to give them fertilizers around them and ensure they are well-nourished. It also makes it hard to water them and look for any weeds, insects, or other types of infestations.

Pruning is very important. You can start by ensuring the leaves that touch the ground and cover the soil where you need to water and feed are removed. To trim off the leaves touching the ground or that are overlapping, use gardening scissors—be careful not to hurt yourself.

You can use gardening gloves as a form of protection as well. You will know you have done an excellent job when you can see around your cabbage plants, you're able to water them, and you can feed them fertilizer with no obstructions.

You need to be able to see the soil bed enough to inspect it for any possible virus infections, worms, or diseases. When you prune your cabbage plants, you may need to remove unhealthy leaves and some healthy-looking ones.

In some cases, you may have either spaced your cabbages too close to each other, or they may have overgrown and are tightly locked. You will then need to remove some cabbages to create the necessary space for proper growth.

This process is often referred to as "thinning." It may seem counterproductive, but it can be necessary, especially when the overcrowding causes your cabbages to not grow properly, attract infestations and other issues.

If you feel terrible about wasting healthy cabbage leaves from pruning or thinning, you can wash them and use them in a recipe! This is a great way to lessen food waste and still benefit from all your hard work.

Watering Cabbages

Cabbage plants are heavy feeders and need a lot of water to grow well. They must consistently have moist soil conditions that keep them fed throughout the day.

However, the soil should not be soaked with water, as they do not tolerate overwatered soil. They need just over an inch of water each week to grow the beautiful lush, yummy, and leafy greens.

You can simplify watering them by giving them water once a week. Always consider your weather conditions; if it has been raining, you may need to skip watering it for the week, depending on how the soil feels and looks.

The first three inches of the soil need to be moist; if it's not, this will indicate that you should water it more. Your watering schedule and amount of water may change yet again when it's very-hot.

That's because the heat will cause water to evaporate quickly from the soil. You can control this or prevent it by using mulch. Add a thick layer of much around your cabbage plants.

Make sure it's around four inches thick to protect your soil well enough, but ensure the mulch is also four inches away from the stem of the cabbage plant. Should extreme hot conditions and evaporation happen faster than average, you can cover the mulch with some plastic.

When watering your cabbages, always water the base and soil of the plant and not the actual cabbage head. This will ensure that the cabbage gets all the water it needs and will help you avoid any infections or diseases caused by dampness on your cabbage plant.

However, it won't necessarily be bad for your cabbage heads to get water. Ensure that you water your cabbages early in the day—this will also give the water gathered in the cabbage enough time to evaporate.

Fertilization For Cabbages

Since cabbages need so much water and nutrients, you cannot avoid feeding them or fertilizing them. If you do, the results may not be great, and you might be disappointed. Therefore, if you want the best results, feed your cabbage plants!

Your soil may have enough nutrients and be fertilized—that's great! However, cabbages typically need extra nutrients to grow well. They need you to fertilize them regularly—this can be weekly to make sure it gets enough.

You can use a well-balanced liquid fertilizer, 10-10-10 will typically be fine. Mix the liquid solution with water—mix one tablespoon of the solution into a gallon of water.

You will then use a cup of this mixed solution for every single cabbage every week or every two weeks. Organic fertilizers should always be your first choice for the best results.

PROTECTING YOUR CABBAGES

Cabbage plants are prone to be threatened by pigeons, worms, moths, and other pests. Since cabbages are such big plants, it might be heartbreaking when just one is damaged. It can feel like such a significant loss, but below, we will share with you some great ways you can protect your cabbage garden.

Extreme Temperatures

Although cabbages are typically resistant to very cold temperatures, they will need some protection. You can do this by covering them with plastic or other covering that keeps them insulated from extremely cold temperatures.

Extremely temperatures can also threaten your cabbages; in this case, you will need to make sure your cabbages have adequate moisture in the soil.

In some extreme heat cases, your cabbage garden may benefit from being shaded giving it a chance to survive the heat damage. Just make sure to avoid this if it is not necessary, as cabbages can tolerate hot temperatures and can be just fine under direct sunlight for long periods.

Protect Cabbages From Pests

Pests such as cabbage root maggots and other worms—which eat your cabbage plants and lay eggs on them—can set you back big time.

However, using collars around the base of your cabbage can significantly reduce the risks of maggots or worms reaching your cabbage plants. It may seem simple and ineffective, but it does help a lot, and it's worth trying.

You may not need to buy special plant collars for your cabbages because you can use some cardboard or other material that won't harm your plants.

You can cut them out in circles - make a straight cut to the hole in the middle to open up and put it around the bottom stem of your cabbage plants. To secure the collar, staple the slit to ensure it won't move or let the pests through.

One of the ways to prevent the maggots is to put the collar around the stem onto the soil bed soon after planting them so you don't give the maggots time to lay eggs around the plant.

To make your collars last as long as possible, you can coat them with wax. Suppose you already have these maggots wreaking havoc in your cabbage garden. In that case, you will need to treat the soil before you use the collars with *Steinernema feltiae* (parasitic nematodes) or another effective treatment.

Birds are another threat to your cabbage garden, unfortunately. You may need to create or buy fencing around your cabbage plants to prevent birds from eating your cabbage or destroying them.

Butterflies can also sit on your cabbages and eat away, so you may further benefit from a kind of fencing that makes it hard for butterflies to access your cabbages.

You can also plant dill or mint around your cabbages to protect them from mites or aphids. Plant hyssop around your garden to protect your cabbages from moths. Hyssop is also very beneficial in stimulating the growth of your cabbages.

You can also plant some thyme next to your cabbage garden to protect them from cabbage worms. That's because thyme acts as a repellent against cabbage worms.

All these types of plants act as repellents and are used as sacrificial plants in some cases, where the pest will rather eat and destroy them instead of the cabbage.

HARVESTING CABBAGES

The time from planting to harvesting typically takes around 60 to 180 days. The time can vary depending on the type of cabbage variety you are planting, the season you are planting in, fertilization, etc.

However, you will know your cabbages are ready to be harvested when the cabbage heads have reached the desired size of when they are meant to be at maturity. It's important to harvest the cabbage heads when they are ready and not beyond that time, as the mature cabbages tend to start splitting when left for too long on the stem.

You can touch and feel the cabbage head to ensure that it's as big as it looks and are ready. Using a knife or scissors, you will cut the cabbage head off the stem.

Make sure you cut at the base of the cabbage stem. To harvest cabbages throughout the year, you will need to plant each cabbage suited for each season.

That's because not all cabbages grow well in all seasons, the good news is that there is a cabbage type to grow for each season, whether in winter, spring, fall, or summer. This also means you will harvest your cabbages in different seasons depending on the type and when you have planted.

After harvesting your cabbage heads, you will need to remove any damaged or dead leaves. Clean the cabbage gently, also checking for pests such as worms and other insects.

You can store your cabbage heads in a plastic bag to help them stay moist and not dry up then place in your fridge.

Once the cabbage is cut, you will need to consume it by day three or in a week at most.

SAVING CABBAGE SEEDS

When cabbages grow, they produce not only cabbage heads and leaves but flowers too. Once you have harvested your cabbages, you may want to grow them again in the following season with the seeds from your current harvest.

You can do so, and it's quite simple, although it requires some patience. Once your cabbage head has fully formed and harvested, you will leave the stem in the ground. Flowers will eventually start growing from it, and the flowers on the stem will have the seeds you need for next season's cabbage garden.

The seeds from the stem will typically be yellow, and the seeds will usually dry and fall to the ground over time. You can either allow this process to happen, or you can harvest the seeds before they dry up and dry them up yourself until they turn brown. Usually, dried cabbage seeds last up to five years.

CHAPTER 5
GROWING YOUR SALAD CARROTS

arrots are a delicious and healthy addition to any diet, and they're also relatively easy to grow. One of the main reasons to grow your own carrots is that you can be sure of their freshness.

Store-bought carrots are often several days old by the time they reach the shelves, and they can lose a lot of their flavor and nutrition in that time. Carrots that you've just pulled from your own garden, on the other hand, will be incredibly fresh and nutritious.

Another reason to grow your own carrots is that you'll have more control over their flavor. By choosing the right variety of carrot and experimenting with different methods of cooking, you can create carrots that are as sweet or savory as you like.

THE RIGHT SOIL FOR CARROTS

Carrots are vegetable plants that can grow pretty much anywhere, and they love lots of sun exposure. They love soil that is clean and free of debris, so make sure your soil is free of rocks.

You must keep rocks out of your garden soil if you want your carrots to shape like carrots and not get twisted, forked or deformed. The root tip of a carrot is very sensitive to obstacles, debris, and rocks in the soil.

The right soil for your carrots will be a bit airy and not too heavy; therefore, avoid clay and compacted soil, as they will limit the growth of your carrot roots. However, soil compaction and an overabundance of rocks can happen in any garden.

Therefore, you will need to constantly keep your soil clean and remove debris when it's present. Use a garden fork to fluff up the soil to prevent compaction; also, make sure you don't damage the carrot root when you do so.

If you have an in-ground type of garden, avoid walking on the soil where you have planted your carrots to prevent compaction. Create small routes you can walk that won't affect the carrot garden.

If you, unfortunately, have mostly compacted soil, no need to worry—you can still make it work by first treating your soil and mixing it up with sand or looser soil. Just make sure to add compost in there as well. If you are unsure what kind of soil you have, it's a good idea for you to test your soil.

This will let you know what type of soil you have, if it's fertile and what added nutrients it may need. Carrot grows best in soil with a pH of 6 to 6.5—an acidic environment will produce a poor harvest.

Carrot Plant Diseases

Carrots have a few common diseases that affect them. For example fungal diseases like leaf spot, which causes dark circle spots on the carrot leaves.

Another is powdery mildew fungus which can cause white spots on leaves and the plant stem causing it to look like cotton. Carrots can get bacterial diseases that cause the yellowing and browning of their leaves.

Usually, it can be easy to spot these diseases and not extremely challenging. Typically, treating common fungal and bacterial diseases is particularly difficult. So the best practice is to prevent them from occurring.

You can avoid disease by ensuring your soil is drained well, not soggy, and the carrot variety of seeds is resistant to such diseases. Weeds tend to bring around bacterial and fungal infections, so you should avoid having them around your carrot garden. If you see any at all, immediately remove the weeds.

One of the challenges with growing healthy and nutritious carrots is preventing forked roots. This is when a carrot develops more than one carrot root form. This defect can be frustrating when you want the conventional-shaped carrots and are doing all the right things to grow the "perfect carrots."

Carrot roots can twist, branch, and appear lumpy in addition to forking. However, while they may look odd and not ideal, these defects don't affect the carrot's nutritional value in your diet.

Overall, if you have done everything right and still happen to harvest carrots that are distorted, you can still enjoy them in your meals.

One of the best ways to prevent deformities is to ensure your soil is free from any obstacles that may force the carrot to change direction in how it grows. Obstacles in the soil can cause your carrots to deform!

HOW TO SOW CARROTS

Correct Season To Plant Carrots

Carrots grow in the cooler season and will likely produce a lousy harvest if you decide to grow them in the warmer season. They are plants for the spring and fall seasons! You can start planting them in early spring for the best results and then harvest them in summer.

Planting Needs And Requirements

Carrot plants, unlike others, don't always like to be trans-planted, so you will need to be careful with how you germinate and transplant them. It's typically a smarter choice to let them grow in the area you first planted or germinated them—this is so you don't disturb them and affect their growing process.

This does not mean you won't be able to germinate them in containers and later plant them in your outside garden. You can still do this by germinating the carrot seeds in biodegradable containers.

These kinds of containers will mean you can take that entire container and put it in the soil where the carrots will grow until harvest. The containers will then biodegrade into the soil! This means you can avoid disturbing the carrot roots and the growing process.

The carrots will then grow successfully until you need to harvest them; however, this is only possible if the soil is fertile enough for the carrots.

Make sure you are transplanting them in good soil. Although carrots may be sensitive to transplanting, it doesn't mean they can't be done successfully!

Carrots typically take around two to three weeks to germinate in nighttime temperatures of 55 °F and daytime temperatures of 75 °F. Therefore, make sure the temperature around your germinating seeds is not below 55 and not above 75 °F at any given time.

To use containers, you can start by placing rich organic matter or soil inside of them and place two to three seeds inside at around an inch deep.

This is done so you can pick the best-growing plant to later transplant or germinate as many carrot seeds as possible. During this stage, it is advised to use an organic fertilizer to encourage growth. You will then lightly water them and ensure the containers drain well and don't cause soggy soil.

Alternatively, you can germinate your carrot seeds by placing them directly in the ground. You will do this by opening an inch-deep row and placing seeds in them and lightly water them.

Spacing And Measurements

The type of garden you choose to have for your carrot plants will determine their growth and how successful the harvest season will be.

That's because the carrot root needs enough space to grow down as much as possible. Containers or raised beds will work, provided they are deep enough for your carrots.

However, there are fewer risks when you use the traditional in-ground garden as there is no limit to how deep the roots can grow. After germinating your carrots in containers for two to three weeks, you can make one-inch-deep rows to two-inch-deep rows, depending on the size of your germinated plant. You will then place the seedlings in rows and space them apart by three to four inches.

MAINTAINING YOUR CARROT GARDEN

Carrots can be easy to maintain, and it not that tricky despite what is commonly assumed. However not making sure the soil is free of debris and not compacted can cost you a lot.

Making sure there are no weeds and the soil has no pests eating at your carrot roots is another important thing you need to look out for. Below, we will share ways you can successfully maintain your carrot crops.

Pruning And Thinning Your Carrots

You will typically need to prune and thin your carrots right after they germinate and the leaves have grown to around two or three inches high. You will need to thin your carrots again once the leaves have grown four inches tall.

Through pruning, you will root out the bad from the good. Another great thing you can do is regularly thin out or shave off the leaves of your carrot plants.

This is done to encourage the plant to give the carrot root most of the nutrients instead of the leaves. Therefore, thinning can benefit your carrots as it encourages the roots to grow larger, longer, and stronger.

The space between your carrots is important, as over-crowding can cause your plants to compete not only for space but nutrients as well. You will generally need to prune and thin your carrot plants when they start crowding: this will help the soil bed be visible for easier inspection for infestation and pest.

Don't wait for the signs; rather, prevent them by constantly monitoring your garden. Additionally, be careful when thinning out your carrot leaves, as this may attract carrot flies. Monitor your garden and protect it should this become a problem.

Watering Carrots

Carrots will need roughly one inch of water every week. However, the amount they need will depend on the weather conditions and rainfall.

When it rains, you will adjust the amount of water needed based on how moist the soil is. When watering your carrots make sure to soak the soil well, as the water needs to penetrate deep enough for the carrot roots. Ensure that the surface of the soil is wet enough and that the roots are well watered.

Fertilization For Carrots

Carrots are sensitive to nitrogen, and if the nitrogen levels in the soil are not balanced or overwhelming, the results can be distressing for any gardener. Too much nitrogen should be avoided.

This is another reason why testing your soil will help prevent any hiccups. When planting carrots, nitrogen levels should be fairly moderate. Most root vegetables like the carrot plant, need a rich amount of potassium and phosphate to grow well.

Therefore, carrots grow best when nitrogen levels are moderate, and potassium and phosphate levels are high.

PROTECTING YOUR CARROTS

It can be frustrating when you finally get to harvest your carrots and pull out your carrots with badly eaten spots that are rotting and smelly.

You could also have missing carrot roots because an animal has taken one. Well, if you have rabbits nearby, this might be your reality. Below, we will share some helpful ways to protect your crops make sure you can enjoy your harvest later.

Extreme Temperatures

Carrots can't tolerate extremely hot weather conditions, that's why it's best to avoid growing them in warmer seasons. Their growth can be affected when it's too hot, and they can develop a very bitter flavor.

When it's very hot, your carrot may benefit from being shaded to protect them from excess heat. Laying mulch around them and on the soil bed will also prevent moisture from evaporation and quick drying.

Although they love growing in cool weather, extreme cold weather conditions can also be harmful your carrot crops. When carrot plants are in a cold environment for too long, this can cause the root to change color and be paler-looking.

You can protect them from extremely cold temperatures by covering them with a mesh or any other covering, such as plastic that controls the temperature around them. Mulch will also warm them up when it's too cold.

Protect Carrots From Pests

When is come to carrots, some of the most damaging pests are carrot flies! They can damage the root with their maggots eating your carrots quietly without even noticing.

The larvae are brought into your soil by carrot flies. Their eggs or larvae typically travel inside the root and damage it. You can prevent this from happening by covering your carrots with some mesh which makes it hard for the flies to access your carrot garden.

For the mesh to work, you will need to ensure that it covers your entire carrot garden with not a single open spot the flies can use as an entry. Another troublesome pest is cutworms—these are especially problematic when you have new seedlings.

They can destroy the new seedlings and set you back big time. To prevent them, you can use a mesh as well from the time you start germinating your carrot seeds, not giving them a chance at all. Better safe than sorry.

They typically look brown and their eggs are brown like moths. The goal is to prevent these moths from landing in your garden to lay their eggs.

You can also use collars at the base of your carrot stem that will sit on the soil bed to prevent the laying of eggs around the carrots. You can further use repellents that can be useful, such as coffee around your plants.

Other types of pests are rodents and even pets. Rabbits, rats, and many more can easily ruin your carrot plants. One of the easiest ways to repel them is by letting your cat or dog roam free around the yard; that will show them not to mess with your garden.

Your cat or dog will likely hunt them, catch them, or make it hard for them to stick around. However, be careful; as your pets could climb, step on, or disturb your plants. You can also put a fence around your garden to protect it from rodents.

Another common pest are roundworms, also called nematodes. You can't see with your natural eye because they are so tiny and microscopic.

They can live in your soil and cause your carrots to fork or deform. They also can lessen your harvest and give your disappointing results. One great way to prevent them is to plant carrot varieties resistant to them.

Another great way to protect your garden from pests is to practice crop rotation and not plant carrots in the same location consistently: pick a different soil or area. This will cause pests to die off or go elsewhere looking for what they need.

HARVESTING CARROTS

From planting to harvesting carrots typically takes around 50 to 80 days. The time can vary depending on the type of carrot variety you are growing, the season you are planting in, fertilization and much.

You will know your carrots are ready when they are around an inch or more in diameter and you start seeing them on the surface of the soil. Their color will also be concentrated and very bright.

If you planted your carrots at the same time, there's no need to be concerned about whether they'll all be ready at the same time. If they aren't all ready, or if some are but others aren't, it could be due to how they were cared for or the soil conditions.

This sometimes happens, but it's easy to avoid if you maintain them well, plant them the right way, and ensure they're in the right soil to start with.

To harvest your carrots, you will need to have a tight grip on the stem or root head and pull. This is generally all you need to do; in some cases where the soil is hard and compacted, you might need to use a fork to soften the soil or pull them out.

Just be careful not to puncture or hurt the carrot roots in the process. Right after harvesting, trim off the leaves, leaving a bit of an inch intact.

You will then clean your carrots by either wiping them clean or rinsing them with water. Immediately store them in the fridge in a clean container with a little water.

Just be careful to change the water often to prevent it from getting cloudy and moldy. With this preservation method, your carrots will remain fresh in the fridge for two weeks or more. However, there are many other ways to preserve them, such as pickling!

SAVING CARROT SEEDS

After harvesting your carrot roots, you can plant the carrot tops for them to produce flowers that have seeds. Therefore, if you want to grow carrots from your harvest, you'll need to keep your carrot tops when you cut your carrot roots or consume them.

After the carrot seeds have flowered, they will grow seeds. You can either let them dry out or harvest them and dry them yourself. Carrot seeds are typically good to use for the next three years.

CHAPTER 6
GROWING YOUR SALAD'S PEPPERS

Peppers are a versatile and flavorful addition to any dish, and there are many different varieties to choose from. Peppers can be enjoyed raw, cooked, or pickled, and they can be used in sweet or savory dishes. Best of all, peppers are relatively easy to grow at home. With a little care and attention, you can enjoy fresh peppers from your own garden all season long.

One of the great things about growing your own peppers is that you can choose from a wide variety of types. If you like spicy food, you can try growing jalapeños, habaneros, or even ghost peppers. Or, if you prefer something milder, you can grow bell peppers or sweet cherry peppers.

There also a number of ornamental pepper varieties that are perfect for adding a splash of color to your garden. No matter what type of pepper you choose to grow, you're sure to enjoy the satisfaction of harvesting your own fresh peppers.

THE RIGHT SOIL FOR PEPPERS

Peppers grow well in moist, fertile soil that is drained relatively well. However, they especially love to grow in sandy loam soil enriched with organic compost and organic matter.

It's also important to ensure that the soil you use for peppers was not recently used for peppers; crop rotation is key here. Due to the nature of their roots being very shallow, they need to be able to spread out as far as they need to.

This is why loose and sandy soil is the best kind for peppers! The easier the roots spread, the bigger, stronger, and more they produce. Peppers also need a neutral pH soil that is around 6.7 to 7.3.

Always test your garden soil, especially ground soil, before using it to ensure it's healthy. However, if you buy soil that is already made for peppers, this might cut out the work for you.

Even if you buy suitable soil, peppers will require feedings to ensure that they grow to their full potential. Like any other vegetable plant, clean your soil beforehand and ensure it's free from pests, debris, and disease.

Pepper Plant Diseases

When deciding which pepper variety you would like to plant, it's always best to use seeds resistant to some of the most common diseases plaguing peppers.

One of the most problematic causes of disease in pepper plants is fungal infections that can wreak havoc on your entire pepper garden. This is especially the case when the garden is overly damp or soaked in water for long periods.

This will naturally draw some problems—not just fungi. Bacterial leaf spots, mosaic virus, powdery mildew, southern blight, sunscald, and blossom end rot are some that can be of concern to you when growing peppers.

Some of the signs your pepper plants could have bacterial leaf spots are yellow spots that will predominantly be on the leaves, and also some browning. Additional signs are leaves that wilt, droop, and die.

With the mosaic virus, your pepper plants will start attracting irritating insects that may cause more damage to your crops. In the case of a mosaic virus, unfortunately, the moment you see these signs, there is not much you can do to save your pepper plants.

With the blossom end rot disease, your pepper plants will cause your pepper fruit to rot; this tends to happen because of poor watering habits and a calcium deficiency.

With all the possible pepper plant diseases out there, the most important thing you can do is prevent them from happening. That's because the moment they take hold of your plants, it can be challenging to save your crop.

One of the ways you can prevent disease is to rotate your crops in your soil. Plant a different vegetable in the same soil each season to introduce various nutrients and minerals to create fertile and healthy soil to prevent and withstand such diseases.

You should keep your garden clean at all times and remove weeds or unknown plants, as they can pass on disease and compete for nutrients. Lastly, have good watering habits, try to keep the days or times consistent, and do not overwater. Keep your garden moist but not damp.

HOW TO SOW PEPPERS

Correct Season To Plant Peppers

Peppers should generally be planted a few weeks to a month after the last spring frost. That's because they grow mainly in warmer seasons; however, they are sown toward the end of a cooler season for the best results. It's incredibly important to plant them at the right time, as the season they are planted and grown in affects how much harvest you get, their color, and their taste.

Planting Needs And Requirements

Pepper seeds need temperatures of around 80 to 90 °F to germinate. The length of time it will take for them to germinate is around a week to two weeks. However, in some cases, it can take as long as 40 days for germination!

Just like carrots, peppers don't like being moved from one soil to another or being transplanted. You can use biodegradable containers to put them in the ground, in containers, or raised beds. This will help you lessen the trauma they experience from transplanting and possibly give you a better outcome.

It's always considered wise to germinate in the soil or area they will grow and be harvested from. It's also advised to plant them in the ground if you want to get as many peppers as possible as there is no limit when it comes to space.

There is more than one method to germinate them pepper seeds. One of the ways you can do this is to soften the seed shell first. This is essentially soaking them in water—some people use water and chamomile tea.

Soaking the seeds will help them germinate faster by cutting down the time it takes for the shell to soften and the sprouting to begin. This is something you can do with most seeds; however, it's particularly helpful to do this with seeds that take long to germinate.

In warm water or chamomile tea (with no sugar, of course!), put your seeds inside and let them soak and soften for around a day or two. You will then take the soft-ened seeds and plant them in your soil at around a quar-ter-inch deep.

Ensure the temperatures are right, and lightly water your containers as needed. The seeds germinate best indoors; this is something you will need to do to ensure they get enough warmth.

Spacing And Measurements

Due to the nature of their shallow roots, peppers need enough space beneath to grow. In some cases, growing peppers in a raised bed of containers may yield fewer peppers, especially the big kind. This can be due to the lack of freedom the root has to spread.

This can typically mean they produce more fruit in a tradi-tional in-ground garden. However, this is not always the case; you can use a container or raised bed, provided that it's deep enough for your pepper roots.

Peppers need to be spaced around 12–18 inches apart for optimal growth. This varies based on the type of pepper you are growing and the maintenance it will need.

When you have your seedlings, you will need to either use the containers they were germinated in or gently remove them from their containers with the stem.

Try not to disturb the roots. In rows, around 18–24 inches apart, dig holes deep enough to accommodate your seedling. Insert your seedlings and cover them with the soil. Water your seedlings as soon as you finish covering them with the soil.

MAINTAINING YOUR PEPPER GARDEN

Growing various kinds of peppers is a fairly straightforward task. Much like every other vegetable plant, they need you to care for them properly for them to grow well.

However, peppers in their seedling and smaller size phase need more careful care because they are quite sensitive to temperature during this time. Even with this, they are very enjoyable to grow, and require the same or similar kind of care, and love as you would give any other vegetable plant.

Pruning And Thinning Your Peppers

If you want peppers that won't disappoint you at harvest time, pruning is one of the most important things you will need to do.

Pruning peppers is important to keep them healthy, to make sure they have no disease and that they give each other space to grow.

However, pruning is also important in how the peppers grow. Some peppers grow into bushy plants, and some grow tall. Bushy plants, in general may seem problematic; however, with peppers, their "bushiness" typically means they will produce more peppers for you.

Therefore, you will need to help control the bushiness your plants may have to influence them to still produce tons of peppers but at the same time to also avoid diseases or overcrowding others. Sometimes, pepper plants may grow to be very tall.

This may seem great, but if your pepper stem has few leaves and it's tall, it might mean less harvest for you. Although this is disappointing, you can somewhat influence your tall peppers to produce more leaves and later produce more peppers.

You will do this by trimming them at the tip of the stem. You should typically make sure that the pepper plant has around five to six leaves left after you have trimmed it.

The growing hormones can concentrate on helping the stem grow taller, but by trimming the stem, you are redirecting the growth to what will produce peppers.

After trimming, the stem will start popping out new leaves that will bring you more peppers in the future.

If you have planted peppers too close to each other or some are too bushy, you can also opt to thin them or replant them elsewhere.

However, this is not advised, as peppers do not like being replanted. It's good to be aware beforehand, so you're not caught off guard if they perish after being replanted.

When pruning, remove the stems or leaves that have diseased, are dying, or wilting. Try to trim the plant at the bottom of the stem to ensure the leaves are not touching the ground as much.

Watering Peppers

When watering, always ensure you water the soil bed, not the actual pepper plant. This ensures that your pepper plant does not get any fungal infections or attract pests. Therefore, keep the actual leaves and plants as dry as possible.

Pepper plants need around an inch of water per week and need you to water them well. The water needs to penetrate deep enough to reach the roots of the pepper plants. You will then adjust your watering schedule, frequency, and quantity of water based on how hot, cold, or moist the soil is.

Fertilization For Peppers

The kind of fertilizer that is well suited for peppers is the organic type. However fertilizer of 5-10-10 can be utilized. Peppers need a lot more potassium and phosphate and half as much nitrogen for them to produce enough fruit.

If there is an overabundance of nitrogen, the pepper plant will produce fewer peppers. Therefore, be careful and intentional when picking your fertilizer for the best results.

You can fertilize the soil in preparation before planting your seedlings; however, it's best to avoid fertilizing immediately after planting. This is so that your seedlings don't focus their energy on growing leafy greens and lose focus on fruit production.

The moment your seedlings start to grow and blossom in the soil you planted them in, you can then fertilize them. Another important thing to remember is to fertilize the soil surrounding your plant and not the pepper plant itself. This means avoiding pouring fertilizer—especially the liquid kind—directed onto your pepper plants.

PROTECTING YOUR PEPPERS

Extreme Temperatures

During cold days, your pepper plants will need help getting and staying warm enough. You cannot simply let them be as they can die from cold weather.

They do not tolerate cold temperatures well at all. Bring them indoors if they are in containers, cover them with a warm cover or plastic, or use a device for plants to keep them warm; for example growing lights.

You could also use cones around your pepper plants; this could work when they are smaller with no produce. The same is true with extremely hot temperatures—peppers don't tolerate scorching temperatures well. Hot weather can make your peppers wilt and look sad, so protecting them is also important.

If the sun exposure is too harsh, you can shade them to give them a break. This will help them tolerate hot temperatures more. Pour mulch all around the garden to keep the soil warm during cold weather and to keep it cool and moist during extremely hot temperatures.

Protecting Peppers From Pests

Peppers are a popular ingredient in many dishes, however at times it can be a challenge protecting peppers from pests. There are a variety of insects that are attracted to peppers, including aphids, beetle larvae, and caterpillars.

These pests can quickly destroy a crop, leaving you with little to show for their efforts. Luckily, there are a few things that you can do to protect their peppers from pests.

To start, choose a pepper variety that is resistant to the type of pests that are common in your area. Next, practice good garden hygiene by removing any dead or dying plants as soon as possible. This will help to prevent the spread of disease.

Additionally, make sure to rotate your crops on a regular basis to avoid allowing pests to build up in one area. Finally, consider using a physical barrier such as row covers to keep pests away from your plants.

By taking these precautions, you can help ensure that your pepper plants remain healthy and productive.

HARVESTING PEPPERS

The time from planting to harvesting peppers typically takes around 60 to 90 days. The time can vary depending on the type of pepper variety you are planting, the season you are planting in, fertilization and much more.

Peppers are ready to be harvested when they have grown to the expected size, are firm, and have their color. However, some people may like harvesting peppers that have not yet fully gotten their color.

It's also important to know that the more you cut off your peppers and harvest them, the more your plant will produce more peppers for you. Don't hang on to every bit of pepper on the plant; afraid you won't have more in the near future. You might get more just by harvesting some.

To harvest your peppers, use a sharp knife or garden scissors to cut off the pepper from the stem. Make sure the pepper is cut with some of the stem intact.

Also, avoid being harsh or ripping off the peppers with your hands. This will cause broken stems, making it challenging for your plant to grow more peppers.

Be gentle! Harvested peppers can last two weeks or more when stored in the fridge inside clean plastic. You can pickle them or use other preservation methods to keep them longer.

SAVING PEPPER SEEDS

Many people enjoy pepper seeds as part of their meals, but what most do not consider is growing their peppers from those very same seeds.

Thankfully, with your fresh harvest, you can avoid buying new seeds. It is advised not to save hybrid seeds, as they will likely not grow the same kind of pepper you expect. Although this is harmless, and can still use their seeds from harvest.

To save seed cut the peppers open and remove the seeds. Spread the seeds out on a paper towel to dry for a few days. Once they are dry, store the seeds in an airtight container in a cool, dark place.

CHAPTER 7

GROWING YOUR SALAD SPRING ONIONS

F or many people, the appeal of growing their own spring onions lies in the ability to have complete control over the gardening process. When you grow your own onions, you can choose what type of onion you want to grow, as well as when and where you plant them.

You can also ensure that your onions are free of chemicals and other pollutants. In addition, home-grown onions tend to be fresher and tastier than store-bought onions.

They also offer a sense of satisfaction that comes from knowing you've produced them yourself. Whether you're a seasoned gardener or a novice, growing your own spring onions is a fun and rewarding experience.

THE RIGHT SOIL FOR SPRING ONIONS

Spring onion plants typically grow in any fertile soil, are drained well, and have rich organic compost. However, they do prefer dark, rich humus soil that has a pH range of

6 to 7. They also need full sun exposure of at least six hours a day.

If you don't have humus soil you can buy the soil and mix it with the one you currently have. However you will need to pay attention to the fertility and run tests to ensure it's the right environment for your spring onions to grow.

Spring Onion Plant Diseases

One of the biggest challenges is dealing with spring onion plant diseases. Common problems include white rot, yellowing leaves, and bulb rot.

White rot is caused by a fungus that attacks the roots, causing the plant to turn yellow and die. Yellowing leaves can be caused by nutrient deficiencies or too much water. Bulb rot is a serious infection that can cause the entire plant to collapse.

In order to prevent these diseases, it is important to water the plants carefully and provide them with plenty of sunlight. If a plant does become infected, it is important to remove it from the garden immediately to prevent the disease from spreading.

Good gardening practices, such as crop rotation and the use of mulch, can help to reduce the risk of disease. In addition, choosing disease-resistant varieties of plants can be an effective way to prevent infections.

Finally, it is important to monitor plants regularly for signs of disease. By taking these precautions, gardeners can help to keep their spring onion crops healthy and disease-free.

HOW TO SOW SPRING ONIONS

Correct Season To Plant Spring Onions

Onions prefer to grow in cool temperatures, so you can plant and grow them in spring or fall for the best results. Although they love cool weather, they do not tolerate extremely cold temperatures too well.

Planting Needs And Requirements

The best temperature to germinate spring onion seeds is between 60 to 78 °F. They may not need any light or sun exposure during the germination period and will sprout in around a week or two weeks.

It's best to germinate them indoors and expose them to outside temperatures bit by bit for a few hours before planting in soil; this helps them acclimatize.

To germinate your spring onions, use a seedling tray with rich humus soil and insert some seeds in each tray at half an inch deep, then cover with soil of around a quarter-inch thickness.

You can then lightly spray the soil with water. During this stage, it's a good idea to start fertilizing the soil they will be planted in.

Spacing And Measurements

Due to the nature of spring onion roots, they can be grown in containers with success. Therefore, you can use containers, raised beds, or an in-ground garden to transplant them.

Sow seedlings in rows and in holes at around two to four inches deep and four inches apart from each other. You will then water them immediately after covering them with soil to wet their roots and start the growing process.

MAINTAINING YOUR SPRING ONION GARDEN

Maintaining your spring onion garden is far from a difficult task; they don't require that much effort and care and will grow strong with little effort when the big things are taken care of and out of the way.

Pruning And Thinning Your Spring Onions

Spring onions are a versatile and easy-to-grow crop that can be harvested at various stages of maturity, from small shoots to full-sized bulbs.

Depending on how you want to use them, you may need to prune or thin your spring onion plants at different times during the growing season. If you're harvesting the onions for their greens, you can start pruning when the plants are about 6 inches tall.

Cut the tallest leaves back to about 4 inches, leaving the smaller leaves to continue growing. If you're harvesting for the bulbs, you'll need to wait until the plants have reached about 8 inches tall before thinning them out.

Transplant the stronger seedlings to other areas of the garden, spacing them about 4 inches apart. You can also start harvesting some of the spring onions at this stage by carefully pulling up outermost bulbs.

Continue thinning and harvesting as needed throughout the season. With a little care, you can enjoy a bountiful harvest of delicious spring onions all season long.

Watering Spring Onions

When watering spring onions, be sure to water deeply and thoroughly. Water should penetrate the soil to a depth of at least six inches.

To test the depth of your watering, stick your finger into the soil; if it feels moist at a depth of six inches, then you've watered sufficiently. If not, continue watering until the soil is moistened to that depth.

Be sure to water in the morning so that the leaves have time to dry before nightfall. This will help to prevent fungal growth and disease.

When watering spring onions, it is important to keep the soil moist but not waterlogged. Onion roots are sensitive to standing water, so it is best to water deeply but less often.

For best results, water in the morning so that the plants have time to dry out before nightfall.

Fertilization For Spring Onions

Fertilization is an important part of growing spring onions. The right fertilizer will provide the nutrients that the plants need to grow healthy and strong.

It is important to choose a fertilizer that is high in nitrogen, as this element is essential for leaf growth. Phosphorus is also important for onion bulbs, so it is worth looking for a fertilizer that contains this nutrient.

In terms of timing, it is best to fertilize the onions when they are first planted, and then again when they begin to bulb up. A controlled-release fertilizer can be helpful, as it will provide a steady supply of nutrients over a long period of time.

The fertilizer well-suited for spring onions will have a 5-10-10 balance of the three important nutrients. With careful fertilization, you can ensure that your spring onions have everything they need to thrive.

PROTECTING YOUR SPRING ONIONS

Extreme Temperatures

Spring onions can tolerate some frost weather conditions, especially when it's only for a short periods. However, your spring onion garden must be covered and shielded in extremely cold temperatures to prevent plant damage.

Spring onions can sometimes tolerate temperatures as low as 25 °F and snowy conditions. Unlike other warm-season vegetables, they are considered quite tolerant of frost.

Extremely hot weather conditions can slow down the growth of the leafy green tops they produce, so you will need to shield them by shading them and ensuring the soil remains moist enough. Using mulch is a great way to ensure they say warm during colder climates and cooler during extreme heats.

Protect Spring Onions From Pests

Unfortunately, spring onions are also very susceptible to pests. The most common pests that attack spring onions are aphids, thrips, and whiteflies. These pests can damage the onion leaves and cause the plant to produce less onion bulbs. However there are a few tips to prevent such pest and many others from attacking your crops.

Plant them in an area with good drainage. Spring onions need plenty of water, but they can't tolerate soggy conditions. A well-drained garden bed is the best place to grow them.

Choose a pest-resistant variety. Some varieties of spring onions are more resistant to pests than others. When choosing a variety to grow, research which ones have a better track record for pest resistance.

Keep the garden clean. Pests are attracted to cluttered and overgrown gardens. Practice good garden hygiene by keeping the area free of debris and weeds. This will help reduce the chances of pests taking up residence in your garden.

Inspect plants regularly. Even if you've taken all the precautionary measures, it's still possible for pests to find their way into your garden. Inspect plants regularly for signs of damage, and take action immediately if you see any evidence of pests.

By following these simple tips, you can help keep your spring onion crop safe from harm.

HARVESTING SPRING ONIONS

Spring onions are one of the first crops to be harvested in the springtime. They are a type of onion that is planted in the fall and overwintered, meaning that they are among the hardiest vegetables.

When spring arrives, the onion plants begin to sprout new green growth. This is the cue for you to begin harvesting the onions.

Harvesting spring onions is can be fun because you can get tons of harvest from just one plant. You can snip off the tops to use in meals, and your spring onion plant can regrow more tops for you to use again.

Typically, this happens twice and sometimes three times. It's advised not to snip off the entire top but only some pieces, as this will allow the plant to keep growing and not stop and die off.

It can typically take around eight weeks to three months for your spring onions to re-grow again ready for harvest.

To harvest your spring onions, use a sharp knife or garden scissors to cut off the green tops, but be careful not to cut too far down. Leave a bit of green, so you don't damage the stem and prevent it from growing more.

Once harvested, clean them up and put them in a clean plastic bag in a refrigerator drawer for two or three weeks.

SAVING SPRING ONION SEEDS

With how delicious spring onions are, you might want to keep growing them. You also might want to control what kind of seeds you plant. In this case, saving seeds from your harvest is a smart choice and will also save you money.

Spring onion seeds are gathered from its flower—we bet you didn't know they bloomed, right? They do, and it's beautiful! Right after your spring onions have grown flow-ers, allow them to start browning and dying.

You will then cut off the head of each flower and remove the seeds, placing them in a glass container if they are already dry. If some are still not fully dry, you can lay them out to dry for longer and store them once they're dry. It's that simple!

CHAPTER 8
GROWING YOUR SALAD RADISHES

Radishes are one of the easiest vegetables to grow, and they are a great option for beginner gardeners. They have a short growing season, so you can enjoy fresh radishes in as little as 4 weeks.

In addition, radishes are relatively low maintenance, and they do not require a lot of space. You can even grow them in containers on your balcony or patio.

Best of all, homegrown radishes are far tastier than the ones you find in the supermarket. They are crisp and crunchy, with a slightly spicy flavor that is perfect for salads or sandwiches.

So why not give growing your own radishes a try? You may be surprised at how rewarding it can be.

THE RIGHT SOIL FOR RADISHES

Radish plants can grow anywhere with fertile soil; they prefer sandy soil with a pH range of about 6.5 to 7. They love organic matter and soil that is enriched with compost.

So your soil needs to be well drained without obstructions or debris like rocks. You will need to prepare your soil, test it, and give it the necessary nutrients to create the right environment for your radish plants.

Radish Plant Diseases

There are many different diseases that can affect radish plants. Some of the most common include leaf spot, white mold, powdery mildew, and downy mildew.

Leaf spot is characterized by small, dark spots that appear on the leaves of the plant. White mold appears as a white, fuzzy growth on the leaves or stems of the plant.

Powdery mildew appears as a white, powdery growth on the surface of the leaves. Downy mildew appears as a gray or white growth on the undersides of the leaves. All of these diseases can cause the leaves of the plant to yellow and drop off. In severe cases, the plant may die.

There are several ways to prevent radish plant diseases. One way is to start with disease-free seed. Another way is to rotate your crops so that radishes are not grown in the same spot every year.

This helps to break the cycle of disease. Another way to prevent radish plant diseases is to water early in the day so that the leaves have time to dry before nightfall.

This helps to reduce the risk of fungal growth. Finally, make sure to remove any infected plants as soon as possible and dispose of them in a way that will prevent the spread of disease.

By following these simple steps, you can help to keep your radish plants healthy and disease-free.

HOW TO SOW RADISHES

Correct Season To Plant Radishes

Radishes grow in the cool season, much like spring onions. They love temperatures of about 40 to 70 °F to grow strong and yield a good harvest. It's best to sow your radish seed a few weeks or months before the last frost.

Planting Needs And Requirements

This vegetable plant is such a super achiever. It usually takes around four days to a week for a seedling to sprout; this is good news as you'll be harvesting them in no time. However, the germination duration depends on the temperature and how deep you plant them.

The deeper they are planted, the longer it takes to see any sprouting signs. Unfavorable temperatures can also delay the sprouting process. The best temperature to germinate radishes is between 40 to 70 °F.

To germinate your radishes indoors, use a seedling tray with rich fertile soil. On the surface, spread out your seeds and cover them with a half-inch thick layer of soil. Alternatively, you can make holes and insert seeds half an inch deep.

Spacing And Measurements

When your seedlings are ready and have around three or four leaves, you can start preparing to transplant them to their permanent home until harvest time. Radishes can be grown in containers, raised beds, or in-ground gardens with no problems.

Make rows in your soil, thin out your radish seedlings, and separate them to line them up evenly. In your soil row, make holes that are one to two inches deep and four to six inches apart. Insert each seedling in its hole and gently cover it up with soil.

Lightly water your soil to jump-start the growing process. Make sure the garden you are transplanting gets direct sunlight for at least six hours daily.

MAINTAINING YOUR RADISH GARDEN

Radishes are not only easy to grow but are a joy to maintain! They grow incredibly fast, and you can rest assured that adhering to the simple instructions below will make you a successful radish gardener.

Pruning And Thinning Your Radishes

The growth rate of radishes can be so quick that you miss out on pruning them. Monitor them consistently, as not cleaning the garden space to prevent disease and check for weeds will ruin your harvest results.

This is especially important when you also want to eat the leaves; as you might have enough before the radishes are ready. In this case, some people trim off the leaves and use them while waiting for the plant to mature.

When you trim the leaves off, you are also stimulating the plant's growth, and it will grow more greens to trim off again. If your radish plants are too close to each other, you might need to thin them out by removing some plants in some sections. This might be needed if the overcrowding is severe.

Watering Radishes

One of the most important things you can do for your radish plants is to water them regularly. The roots of radish plants grow quickly, and they need a consistent supply of moisture to stay healthy. Water your radishes early in the morning, using just enough to wet the soil without leaving any standing water.

Depending on the weather and the size of your plants, you may need to water every day or every other day. If the leaves of your radishes begin to wilt, that is a sign that they are not getting enough water.

Give them a good soaking, and then check the soil regularly to make sure it is not too dry. By giving your radishes the right amount of water, you will be rewarded with a bountiful harvest of crisp and flavorful roots.

Fertilization For Radishes

You will need to fertilize the soil before you plant your radishes. The kind of fertilizer to use should be a 16-20-0 kind. Radishes typically don't require more fertilization after they are planted in fertile soil.

This means you will need to take care and maintain your soil well enough, as any additional nutrients won't be needed. Avoid an overabundance of nitrogen in your soil if you want the radish bulbs at harvest unless you are simply planting radishes for just the greens.

PROTECTING YOUR RADISHES

Extreme Temperatures

Radish plants are among some of the most frost-resistant crops out there. They hold up well and tolerate really cold temperatures of as low as 20 °F.

Although cold temperatures can kill off their leaves, the radish is rarely affected to the point where it dies. You can rest assured knowing that once the frost is over, your radish leaves will grow back.

However, you can attempt to protect your radish leaves by covering them to keep them warm by using mulch around them to lock the heat in. The radish plant will not grow bulbs properly in hot temperatures, such as those between 80 to 85 °F.

Therefore, prolonged hot temperatures will result in unimpressive harvest results. In temporary heat waves, you can shade your plants, water them if the soil is dry, and add mulch around them to prevent extreme water evaporation.

Protect Radishes From Pests

Radishes are a popular garden crop that can be easily grown in most climates. However, they are also susceptible to pests, which can damage the roots and ruin the crop. The most common radish pests include aphids, leafhoppers, and root maggots.

To protect your radishes from these pests, it is important to take preventative measures. One way to do this is to choose a variety of radish that is resistant to pests. Another way to prevent pests is to keep your garden clean and free of debris.

This will help to reduce the number of places where pests can hide and lay their eggs. Row covers can be used to keep pests from getting to the plants, and regular inspection can help to identify problems early on. Finally rotating crops in the same soil will also avoid some of these issues.

HARVESTING RADISHES

Harvesting radishes can take anywhere between three weeks to two months. You could easily ruin your harvest if you are unaware of how quickly radishes grow or aren't keeping track of the timeline.

Leaving them too long in the ground can create problems, so you must harvest when it's time to harvest. Sometimes, setting calendar reminders is helpful because you don't want to mess up growing this simple and easy-growing vegetable.

Like most vegetable plants, you harvest radish greens to use in your meals, soups, or stews. After harvesting radish leaves, clean them and store them in a plastic bag in the refrigerator.

You can harvest radish bulbs using a garden spade to gently dislodge them from the soil, especially in compacted dry soil. However, in most cases, they should be easy to pull out by hand with the right soil.

You can clean them up, chop off the leaves, chop off the roots, place the bulbs in a clean container or plastic, and refrigerate them for up to three weeks.

SAVING RADISH SEEDS

To get seeds from radishes, you will need to let your radish plant sit in the soil to mature until they flower and produce pods. In the pods, you will find the seeds you need to store and use to plant more radishes.

The pods are edible; however, it's not common for them to be eaten. Once the plant produces pods, you can let the pods and the plant dry out until you can feel and hear the seeds moving around. By this time, the pods would have changed color from green to brown and will have dried out.

You can either wait for the pods to dry themselves or cut out the pods with their stems to hang and dry in the sun. You can then collect your seeds in a clean container and save them for later use.

CHAPTER 9
WHY GROW YOUR OWN VEGETABLES?

G ardening is more than just for eating delicious nutrient-dense foods, although this is a good motivation to start gardening. In this chapter, you will learn all the fantastic ways gardening benefits you physically, mentally, financially, and socially.

THE PHYSICAL HEALTH BENEFITS OF GARDENING

It Increases Vitamin D and C in Your Body

According to a 2014 study by the National Institute of Health through Sustain Web, gardening can increases vitamin D in the body; as a result, this increases vitamin C absorption.

With gardening, you will typically spend more time outdoors and be more exposed to sunlight than usual. Vitamin D is especially important as you age for stronger bones as it aids in absorbing vitamin C, strengthening your immune system, and extending your life.

This is important because as we age, we receive less sun exposure; as a result, we develop vitamin D insufficiency. We are generally less motivated to spend time outside as digital items, the internet, TV, and other technologies become more prevalent in our lives keeping us indoors.

There's the argument that you could take vitamin D supplements, but not everyone enjoys them, and some people negatively react to them. The best part about sunshine is that it is completely free and can help you feel better in your body by reducing inflammation. All those aching joints and muscles will appreciate and thank you.

It Helps You Stay Active

Gardening requires physical activity and can greatly contribute to alleviating body stiffness and inflammation from not being active. Keeping active helps you live longer and build up a stoner immune system.

According to *Harvard Health Publishing* in 2018, gardening for 30 minutes can burn between 135 to 189 calories. You're doing something fun, relaxing, healthy, and burning calories. Staying fit is a challenge for many worldwide because exercising isn't necessarily a fun experience but a much-needed one.

Gardening could be a fantastic alternative if you don't like dedicating time to an exercise plan, sweating, and going to the gym. On the contrary, you may be unable to complete particular exercises, or have limitations that restrict you from being as active as you would like.

If this is you, gardening presents a fairly easy way to be active. Although this activity varies among people, your activity can still help you lose calories promoting better health.

Staying active is not only good for weight loss or weight maintenance but also for keeping your joints and muscles strong. The movements you will be making and the efforts will improve the strength of your arms, legs, and any body part supporting you while gardening.

It Can Decrease Your Risk of Developing Dementia

According to a 2006 study on the lifestyle factors and risks of dementia, gardening can decrease your risk of developing dementia by 36% (Simons et al., 2006). This means you can potentially decrease risks by doing a very rewarding hobby that not only benefits your health but feeds you healthy foods.

For those in old age or those in their midlife years, preventing dementia is important. Many people around the world are constantly searching for ways to not only prevent dementia but cure it.

However, science does prove that you can reduce your risks with gardening! With this information in mind, wouldn't you jump at the thought of starting your garden? Many definitely would, as it's not only easy once you understand it but also so rewarding.

It Will Help You Increase Overall Health

Since you will be growing your vegetables, healthy food becomes easily accessible and available for you to eat. By eating healthy foods, you will be boosting your health by consuming more nutrients from nutrient-dense foods.

You will further be able to control the growing process, which means less to no pesticides and other dangerous chemicals. For example, if you need to consume various types of vegetables for nutritional and vitamin benefits each day.

Growing your salad vegetables will make it easier to follow and stick to your diet, as you will have them readily available to eat when they grow in your yard. Overall, gardening helps you improve your health in more ways than one.

As you can see, there are various benefits, and all of these combined can make a substantial difference in how you feel—especially the quality of your life.

THE MENTAL HEALTH BENEFITS OF GARDENING

It Boosts Your Mood

Being in the garden can be quite therapeutic, so much so that you can see noticeable improvements in your mood. For some people, gardening is an outlet to decrease stress.

Nature has a way of making you feel more relaxed, at peace, and positive. It can be very healing! If you feel stressed or uneasy, you can head out to your garden and start maintaining it as a distraction or a way to cope.

This time you spend touching and looking at nature will help you cope with your feelings. Although this may be a temporary solution to most life stressors, it sure is a great tool to feel better when you need to, and it's healthy.

It Can Help You Calm Down After Traumatic Events

Unfortunately, stress is part of many people's lives, and traumatic events can happen to just about anyone at any time. We have all tasted it and wish never to experience it again. This is especially true as we age.

We may need more medical care and medicine, and we discover our bodies can't function as they did before. Gardening is an activity that can take your mind off the current problems you may have. By doing it habitually, you can train your mind and body to relax more.

Therefore, always remember that if you are going through stressful situations, using gardening as a coping mechanism can help you lower the stress hormone cortisol.

It Can Aid You in Recovering From Addiction

The beauty of gardening is that it can distract the mind and calm your nerves. This is important for those who may be recovering from any addiction. It's quite common for some addiction recovery facilities to use gardening or horticultural therapy in their programs.

THE FINANCIAL BENEFITS OF GARDENING

The Very Affordable Initial Cost

According to a 2021 publication by the National Gardening Institute, average households who harvest from their gardens have a good return on their investment (Knerl, 2021).

When you begin gardening, you won't need to spend a huge amount of money to get started; depending on how "fancy" you want your garden to be.

Some people garden successfully without half the common gardening tools; some make their compost because it's quite easy to do. Seeds are very cheap and affordable, considering the harvest you get.

As you grow in your gardening experience, you will quickly see just how few things you need, but you might also want to get more technical, like a moisture reader. However such equipment and added expenses aren't necessary for a successful garden.

You'll Get More Than You Need

The harvest from your garden will far outweigh any financial investment you made. That's because you will get vegetables for the next few months and sometimes more than a year. All this is great, but it will be bad if you let it all go to waste.

You can do charitable work and donate some; you can sell some or learn various vegetable preservation methods. With chili peppers, for example, if you plant enough seeds, you could have a whole yard filled with them—not knowing what to do with them all.

You Can Save Money on Expensive Vegetables

Some vegetables are generally pricey in most stores and vegetable markets—this can be disheartening when you love eating them. However, when you grow them yourself, you will likely save quite a lot of money and have a high return on investment.

This is especially true for scarce crops in your area, as this scarcity can make them expensive. You can do this by first looking into what you usually eat more during a month.

You can plant vegetables that specifically cater to your diet or supplement the vegetables you buy by growing them yourself. This will mean having a lot of what you need, and with the proper preservation methods, you can enjoy your harvest for a long time.

This means that the harvest you get from planting in one season could supplement your diet or eliminate the need to buy the usual stuff for quite a long time—possibly even months with careful planning and execution.

You can plant and grow most of your vegetables and live off them. This might seem impossible, but it's not! Many people lived these ways years ago, and some still do today. As the years go by, inflation changes and food gets more expensive.

It would benefit you if you could start seed saving, especially seeds with a long shelf life. You can look at these seeds as "assets" because they are. They will feed you and are an investment for the future. Invest in pickling jars and plastic containers to preserve your seeds cheaply.

THE SOCIAL BENEFITS OF GARDENING

It Can Help You Connect With Loved Ones More

Gardening together with a loved one can help you experience each other differently. People are different in various situations, and that's why laughing together also helps strengthen connections between loved ones.

By gardening in a relaxing environment, you are both in a good mood. Gardening also brings you together by sharing the same interests. This brings you closer even more as you can relate to each other in a more personal way.

It fosters intimacy and vulnerability, as you both will be responsible for growing a life and learning from each other as your plants grow.

It Will Help You Do More Charitable Work and Help Others

Through gardening, you will be equipped with skills that can change lives. There are people out there that can escape the claws of poverty by gardening, so it would be a rewarding experience to help them out.

You can do charity drives and give some of your harvests away. Your efforts can give someone a meal and keep someone in good health. You can further participate in community gardening and help yourself and the people around you who have local organic fresh produce.

You can reach out to some community members who may benefit from a community garden and reach out to some of your interested gardening friends. By coming together to grow vegetables, you will increase your odds of success, as there are more hands and minds to maintain the garden.

This can seem like an overwhelming task, but it's possible with the help of many hands. Since this is a community and charitable work, many big brands and companies might be willing to lend a hand.

If you need any supplies or resources, you could always pitch the idea of financial assistance to them as part of their community outreach program.

It Exposes You to Possible New Friends and Gives You a Sense of Belonging

When you start gardening, you join an amazing community of other fellow gardeners from all over the world. You will quickly notice just how supportive this community can be.

Whether online or in person, people who are into gardening will find you interesting and soon want to keep you around for lots of gardening talk. This is helpful when you are mostly an indoors person, cannot move around due to disabilities, or may not have many friends.

You can always seek out some friends in the community, and it's easier to connect with them because you already have something in common.

It Will Ease and Reduce Loneliness

Getting new gardening buddies can fill up your time with conversations and companionship with other gardeners. Even better, there are gardening communities for various people, such as the less abled, introverted, extroverted, moms, men, children, and more.

You can find support and form close connections with those who not only have the same interest in gardening as you but people very similar to you. Besides finding support from fellow gardeners, gardening will truly give you the ability to clear your mind for quite a while.

Being so concentrated and in the moment can help you immensely curb feelings of loneliness. This is especially true in community gardening situations. Being in nature and gardening with others will positively impact you.

CHAPTER 10
GLOSSARY

Acidic

Something that forms or becomes acid and has a pH of less than 7.

Aeration

The act of circulating air through a garden, soil, and plants.

Aged manure

Old manure that has matured through a long period by letting it sit in a container.

Alkaline

Something that contains alkali and has a pH above 7.

Aphids

Tiny insects which consume the liquid plants produce such as sap.

Bacteria

A microorganism that causes disease and, at other times, improves the well-being of an organism.

Biodegradable

Something that can decompose into the soil and not harm the soil or other living organisms in it.

Blood pressure

The pressure that is produced by blood as it moves through a circulatory system.

Blunt

Something that is not sharp but softer around its edges and unable to penetrate through something.

Bulb

A plant's fruit or organ grows in soil right above its roots and is typically edible when it's a vegetable plant.

Bushy

Something that is overgrown or grows to be dense, big, and has lots of leaves.

Cabbage loopers

An insect or moth tends to be found crawling and laying eggs on cabbages. This insect is a cabbage pest that destroys crops.

Calcium carbonate

Insoluble chalk is natural and white. This is also called ground limestone.

Collar

A round object is used to cuff the base of a plant to protect it from pests such as worms and maggots.

Compaction

The compression of soil particles removes air pockets and hardens the soil. It is considered harmful when gardening and wants to achieve successful results.

Companion planting

Planting two or more plants next to each other is protective of each other to avoid disease and pests. It can improve harvest results and improve growth.

Compost

A combination of biodegradable plants, objects, or waste that has been mixed to rot and build up nutrients necessary to soil health and fertility.

Container garden

A garden of plants grown in a pot that holds soil.

Crop rotation

Crop rotation is the practice of planting different crops sequentially on the same plot of land to improve soil health, optimize nutrients in the soil, and combat pest and weed pressure.

Cutworms

A damaging and destructive moth larva, this is a vegetable pest that is found in soil and on plants.

Debris

Remains or objects in the soil, such as rocks and previously dead crops, need to be removed to maintain the health of your garden.

Dementia

A mental illness or disorder that causes memory loss and brain injury can affect a person's reasoning.

Drainage

The process by which liquids or water is expelled from something, such as soil.

Drilling tractor

A gardening sowing machine that drills holes into the ground and helps a gardener avoid manual soil drilling to plant his plants.

Ecosystem

Different biological organisms interact with each other to maintain an environment.

Evaporation

Water that turns into vapor.

Fertile soil

Soil that is healthy enough to give plants all nutrients they need to grow successfully until harvest.

Fertilization

Making soil fertile through the use of fertilizers.

Frost

Ice crystals can form on plants when temperatures are freezing or too cold.

Fungus

Living organisms feed on other living organisms and create mold or discolored plants when present. They can destroy plants and cause disease.

Germinate

When a plant starts to grow out of a shell and form shoots or leaves.

Harvest

A collection of mature and ripe plants and their fruit. It's when your plants have matured and you collect them from their stems.

Heart rate

How fast or slow are your heartbeats. It's a number or calculation which determines the heart's speed.

Humus

Decomposed organic matter consists of soil and compost.

Hybrid seed

Seeds have been altered and are offspring of two different types of seed varieties of the same plant.

Mesh

A material you lace over your garden plants that protects them from insects and pests.

Minerals

Substances are naturally occurring and are needed to produce fertile soil and healthy plants.

Moisture

Dampness is caused by diffused water or liquid.

Mulch

Decayed matter, such as compost is placed on the surface of the soil to lock moisture in or protect the soil from harsh weather conditions.

Nitrogen

A nutrient is needed to give plants their green color and healthy leaves.

Nutrients

Elements that feed plants the necessary food they need to grow.

Organic matter

Decomposed humus is in the soil and is essential in growing healthy vegetables.

Organic produce

Food that has been made or grown without the use of chemical alterations.

Pesticides

Organic or chemical substances used to kill or repel insects and other pests in a garden.

Pests

Living organisms are destructive to a garden and must be repelled or prevented from reaching plants.

pH

A chemistry figure which communicates a scale of alkalinity or acidity. It helps you know how alkaline or acidic soil is.

Phosphate

Phosphoric acid is a salt that is needed for the health of the soil.

Positive Aging

The ability to age with good wellness and health.

Potassium

A nutrient that helps plants grow and is essential in their entire life cycle.

Pruning

Maintain a garden by cutting or trimming dead or potentially unwanted parts of a plant.

Roots

The bottom stingy and firm bits of a plant grow and stretch into the soil. They absorb the nutrients and water for a plant's needs.

Seedling

A small and recently germinated plant that is ready to be planted.

Soggy

A mushy, soft, and overly damp area such as soil.

Soilless

Matter which seeds can be grown in and is an alternative to soil.

Sowing

The act of planting, drilling, or scattering a seed onto or into the soil to grow.

Sprout

When a plant produces its first shoots or leaves.

Stem

The structure of a plant that supports all its branches, leaves, and fruit.

Thinning

Separating seedlings clumped together or removing some overcrowded plants from the soil to space out your garden to give others the chance of growing properly.

Transplanting

When you take a plant from one soil, area, or tray into another area or garden, this is also known as replanting it into another space.

CHAPTER 11
ACKNOWLEDGEMENTS

This book would not be possible without our team's expertise, experience, and dedication at Green Roots. To our team members Charles Craig, Annie Hayford, Jessica Reid, Adam Spencer, and Nicole Robinson.

Thank you for your contributions to this book. Your commitment to touching lives and helping communities grow their gardens is unparalleled. This book is made up of more than 20 years of collective gardening knowledge, experiences, insight, and passion.

We are all so thrilled to have this compilation of insightful and useful garden guides that will helps so many gardeners all over the world.

AFTERWORD

There is no doubt that starting your own garden is rewarding! It truly can transform your life in ways you have never imagined before. Your health can be improved, and your overall well-being can flourish.

If gardening does not drastically positively impact you, it will at least improve some things about you and your life. Why are we at Green Roots so sure of this? Well, it's in science! It has been proven that gardening is a therapeutic hobby and leisure activity.

We have personally been impacted by gardening in our lives and could give many stories on how over the years, gardening has achieved this.

Most importantly, we see firsthand how gardening impacts other people through the community of people we help and empower daily. Their lives are changed; they have a better outlook on life and feel better too.

We took on the challenge to write this book to crush the stigma that growing vegetables successfully requires conventional space, tools, and equipment which can be very costly.

Not only has gardening been made to seem like such a difficult thing, but the various books and guides written to "make it easy" continuously miss the mark.

This book is meant to be something easy for you to read, understand, and refer back to whenever you face a gardening challenge. It's written in simple English to help you demystify the idea that gardening is all about fancy jargon and sounding very "expert life."

Becoming an expert in this amazing gardening community is great, especially when you can help others. However, being an expert becomes useless when others cannot understand your information and experience when your "tips and tricks" are not actionable.

This book will give you all you need to know; it may cover a handful of staple salad vegetables, but the knowledge it gives you will extend to any other plant you might want to grow. This knowledge is not only valuable but incredibly timeless.

You can look back decades from now and still be able to use this book. Why? The very basics of gardening do not change. Once you know how to plant and grow your own vegetables, you don't need to start scrambling to learn how to do it from scratch.

It's like riding a bike; you won't look back when you grasp how to do it. Therefore, this book will become one of those books you can use many years from now.

At Green Roots, we aim to help gardeners grow as many vegetables as possible with ease and confidence. This is why we covered various topics that extend far beyond the "norm" in a vegetable guidebook.

We did this with you in mind. Knowing that you may be a beginner, we wanted to give you all the details you will need to start your garden, maintain it and harvest. Below are some great and key takeaways:

Types of Gardens

You now know that there are so many possibilities! Even if you don't have enough yard space to start your garden, you can easily start in containers and improvise where needed.

You learned that although you can do this, containers may give you undesirable results at harvest time for some plants that require deep roots.

You have gained a tremendous amount of knowledge of the advantages and disadvantages of any of the three different kinds of gardens: a container garden, raised bed garden, and an in-ground traditional garden.

Preparing the Soil

One of the things most new gardeners neglect when starting their garden is their soil. They do this by willfully being oblivious and simply buying compost and fertilizer without wanting to know their soil.

However, you now know the importance of understanding the kind of soil you have, as the soil and its fertility are crucial in a plant's ability to grow and give you as much fruit as possible. You learned the various ways to prepare your soil, improve it, maintain it, and protect it from problems.

Deciding What to Grow

Many new gardeners buy seeds and start planting without first understanding their "why" for starting the garden. This helps you determine what kind of vegetables to grow and focus on for the best results.

Why waste time on a vegetable that won't improve your life the most? In this book, you learned exactly how to determine which vegetable plants you will need to plant.

You learned that it would be based on your individual needs and no one else's unless you are gardening for a cause bigger than yourself.

Sowing Techniques

You learned that sowing methods and techniques could vary depending on the kind of garden you are planting and how big you want it to be.

This knowledge equipped you with a good understanding of the techniques and why they would work or not work in your type of garden. Each sowing technique is different, yet all of them can be used in different scenarios.

You are now more knowledgeable about which sowing technique best suits which type of garden. This knowledge will help you avoid time-consuming mistakes and financial loss due to wrong sowing techniques.

Growing Your Salad Vegetables

The biggest and most important thing you learned in this book is found in each vegetable planting guide for cucumbers, peppers, tomatoes, cabbages, radishes, and spring onions.

The guides go in-depth with the gardening process for each of these vegetables. You surely feel empowered to take care of your life and make the best decisions for yourself.

That's because the guides give you very actionable steps from the moment you germinate the seed to harvesting. You will now be able to get your daily salad vegetables right from your living environment without needing to go to the store. This makes your life very convenient and healthier!

The Benefit of Growing Your Own Fruit and Vegetables

We explored the many ways you can benefit from starting your garden and how it can change your life. It's scientifically backed that gardening can improve your life mentally, physically, socially, and financially.

We discussed affordable and cheap gardening and how you get more value for money than if you bought vegetables from a store. This is exciting as it helps give you valid reasons to explore gardening because it's worth trying in every way.

The simplistic nature of this book, its advice, and its instructions will help any beginner gardener thrive and have a successful garden. It will help you see how simple gardening is, how rewarding it is, and how it can improve your life. We truly hope you'll discover the joy and satisfaction that comes from cultivating a thriving, harmonious vegetable garden and would love to share this experience with you via our Facebook gardening community - **facebook.com/groups/greenroots/**

Now that you are well-equipped to grow a successful garden, we would love it if you could give us an honest review of this book. Your feedback and thoughts help us know if we have done a good job at helping you improve your gardening skills. Simply share those in the reviews/comments section of your purchased retailer, and we will surely be on the lookout for them.

"Garden is not just a hobby, but a way of life" - Green Roots

ALSO BY GREEN ROOTS

Fruit and Veggies 101 - Vegetable Companion Planting: Companion Guide On How To Grow Vegetables Using Essential, Organic & Sustainable Gardening Strategies

Fruit & Veggies 101 - The Winter Harvest: Gardening Guide On How to Grow the Freshest & Ripest Winter Vegetables (Perfect for Beginners)

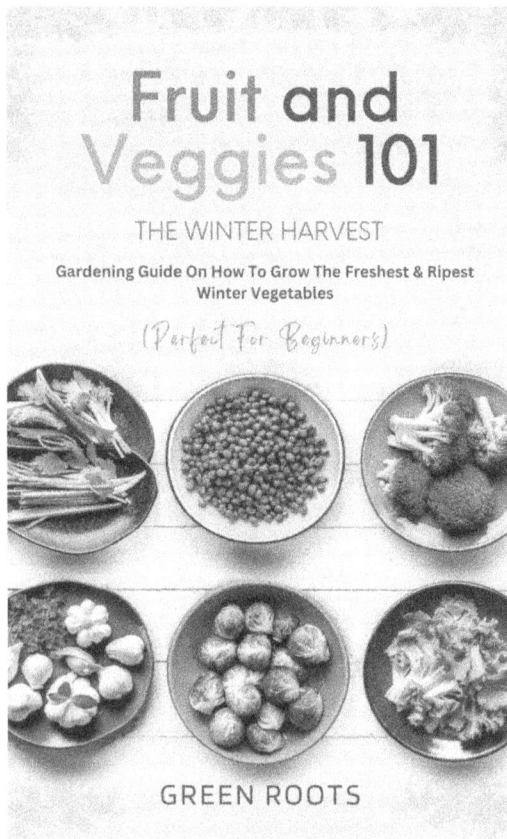

Fruit and Veggies 101

THE WINTER HARVEST

Gardening Guide On How To Grow The Freshest & Ripest Winter Vegetables

(Perfect For Beginners)

GREEN ROOTS

Fruit & Veggies 101 - Summer Fruits: Gardening Guide On How to Grow the Freshest & Ripest Summer Fruits (Perfect for Beginners)

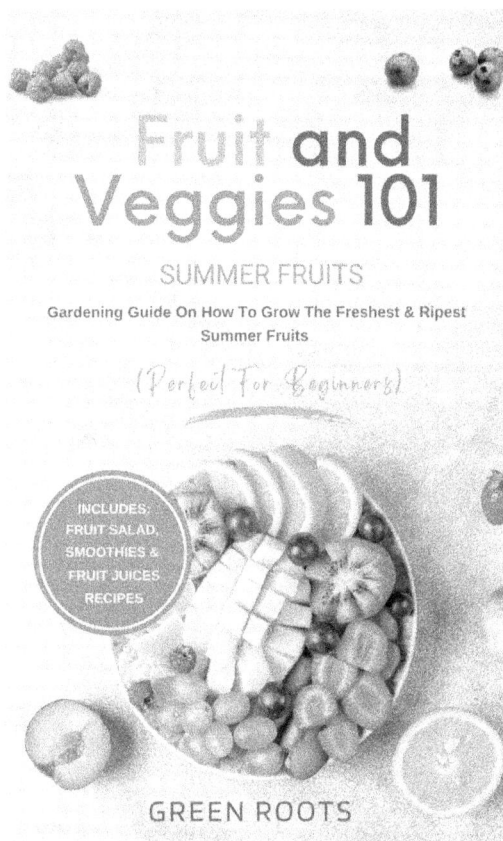

Fruit and Veggies 101

SUMMER FRUITS

Gardening Guide On How To Grow The Freshest & Ripest Summer Fruits

(Perfect For Beginners)

INCLUDES:
FRUIT SALAD,
SMOOTHIES &
FRUIT JUICES
RECIPES

GREEN ROOTS

BIBLIOGRAPHY

10 Reasons to Grow Your Own Organic Food. (2016, February 2). Grow a Good Life. https://growagoodlife.com/grow-your-own-organic-food/

Andrew. (2020, April 23). *What Tools Do I Need To Start a Vegetable Garden? - Gardening FAQs.* Quickcrop Blog. https://www.quickcrop.co.uk/blog/what-tools-do-i-need-to-start-a-vegetable-garden/

Asher, B. (2011). *What Is the Best Fertilizer for Cucumbers? | Hunker.* Hunker. https://www.hunker.com/13427375/what-is-the-best-fertilizer-for-cucumbers

Bailey, V. (2018, December 15). *What Not to Plant Near Cucumbers.* Home Guides | SF Gate. https://homeguides.sfgate.com/not-plant-near-cucumbers-33318.html

Balogh, A. (n.d.). *Garden Soil: How to Prepare Your Soil for a Garden - Garden Design.* GardenDesign.com. Retrieved June 27, 2021, from https://www.gardendesign.com/soil/

Benefits of Community Growing. (n.d.). Www.edibleestates.co.uk. http://www.edibleestates.co.uk/benefits-of-community-growing/

Blando, M. (n.d.). *How Much Sun Does a Cucumber Plant Need?* Homeguides.sfgate.com. https://homeguides.sfgate.com/much-sun-cucumber-plant-need-52857.html

Boeckmann, C. (2021, March 25). *Vegetable Gardening for Beginners.* Old Farmer's Almanac. https://www.almanac.com/vegetable-gardening-for-beginners

Borge, A. (2014, April 24). *The Financial Benefits of Starting a Vegetable Garden.* DebtHelper.com. https://debthelper.com/blog/2014/04/financial-benefits-starting-vegetable-garden/

Campbell-Preston, C. (2016, September 12). *Why Gardening is Great For Your Mental Health and Wellbeing | Capital Gardens.* Capital Gardens. https://www.capitalgardens.co.uk/blog/gardening-great-mental-health-wellbeing/

Castillo, E. (2016, May 7). *How much salad should you be eating each day?* PCOSbites. https://pcosbites.com/2016/05/07/how-much-salad-should-you-be-eating-each-day/

Domoney, D. (2019a, March 8). *Expert guide to soil.* David Domoney. https://www.daviddomoney.com/expert-guide-to-soil/

Domoney, D. (2019b, March 11). *Beginner's Guide to Growing Fruit and Veg.* David Domoney. https://www.daviddomoney.com/beginners-guide-to-growing-fruit-and-veg/

Domoney, D. (2019c, May 13). *Benefits of Gardening for Mental Health.* David Domoney. https://www.daviddomoney.com/benefits-garden-ing-mental-health/

Druff, K. V. (2021, February 28). *8 Amazing Social Benefits of Gardening.* Bunny's Garden. https://www.bunnysgarden.com/social-benefits-of-gardening/

Ferrandino, F. (2014, April 25). *How to Prune Tomatoes.* FineGardening. https://www.finegardening.com/article/pruning-tomatoes

Gardening: Invest in guaranteed growth in your own backyard. (2009, April). Cappersfarmer.com. https://www.cappersfarmer.com/yard-and-garden/gardening-invest-in-guaranteed-growth-in-your-own-backyard/

George, H. (2020, August 29). *Identify, Prevent, and Treat Common Cabbage Diseases | Gardener's Path.* Gardener's Path. https://gardenerspath.com/how-to/disease-and-pests/common-cabbage-diseases/

Gibson, A. (2012, November 27). *Guide to Growing Spring Onions: Every-thing you need to know!* The Micro Gardener. https://themicrogarden-er.com/guide-to-growing-spring-onions/

Gillihan, S. J. (2019, June 19). *10 Mental Health Benefits of Gardening | Psychology Today United Kingdom.* Www.psychologytoday.com. https://www.psychologytoday.com/gb/blog/think-act-be/201906/10-mental-health-benefits-gardening

Go, G. (2014). *7 Surprising Financial Benefits of Gardening.* US News & World Report; U.S. News & World Report. https://money.usnews.com/money/blogs/my-money/2014/05/07/7-surprising-financial-benefits-of-gardening

Growing Cabbages & General Cabbage Planting Tips. (n.d.). Bonnie Plants. https://bonnieplants.com/how-to-grow/growing-cabbage/#:~:text=Like%20most%20vegetables%2C%20cabbage%20needs

Hagen, L. (2019). *12 Gardening Tools to Buy - Essentials for Beginners - Garden Design.* GardenDesign.com. https://www.gardendesign.com/how-to/tools.html

Haifa Group. (2018, March 11). *Crop Guide: Tomato.* Haifa Group. https://www.haifa-group.com/tomato-fertilizer/crop-guide-tomato

Hansen, J. (n.d.). *The Easiest Fruits and Vegetables to Grow for Beginners.* GardenTech.com. Retrieved July 11, 2021, from https://www.garden-tech.com/blog/gardening-and-healthy-living/8-easy-to-grow-fruits-and-veggies

Harvard Health Publishing. (2018, August 13). *Calories burned in 30 minutes for people of three different weights - Harvard Health.* Harvard Health; Harvard Health. https://www.health.harvard.edu/diet-and-weight-loss/calories-burned-in-30-minutes-of-leisure-and-routine-activities

Hayes, K. (2017, June 14). *5 Health Benefits of Gardening and Planting.* AARP. https://www.aarp.org/health/healthy-living/info-2017/health-benefits-of-gardening-fd.html

Heirloom Organics. (n.d.-a). *How to Grow Cucumbers | Guide to Growing Cucumbers.* Www.heirloom-Organics.com. Retrieved July 18, 2021, from http://www.heirloom-organics.com/guide/va/guidetogrowingcucumbers.html

Heirloom Organics. (n.d.-b). *How to Grow Tomato | Guide to Growing Tomatoes.* Www.heirloom-Organics.com. Retrieved July 17, 2021, from http://www.heirloom-organics.com/guide/va/guidetogrowingtomato.html

How to Grow Cabbage| Guide to Growing Cabbage. (n.d.). Www.heirloom-Organics.com. Retrieved August 2, 2021, from http://www.heirloom-organics.com/guide/va/guidetogrowingcabbage.html

How to Grow Carrots | Guide to Growing Carrots. (n.d.). Www.heirloom-Organics.com. Retrieved August 5, 2021, from http://www.heirloom-organics.com/guide/va/guidetogrowingcarrots.html

How to Grow Pepper | Guide to Growing Peppers. (n.d.). Www.heirloom-Organics.com. Retrieved August 5, 2021, from http://www.heirloom-organics.com/guide/va/guidetogrowingpeppers.html

How to Grow Radishes - Gardening Tips and Advice, Vegetable Seeds and Plants at Burpee.com. (2019). Burpee.com. https://www.burpee.com/gardenadvicecenter/vegetables/radishes/all-about-radishes/article10099.html

How to Grow Radishes | Guide to Growing Radishes. (n.d.). Www.heirloom-Organics.com. Retrieved August 5, 2021, from http://www.heirloom-organics.com/guide/va/guidetogrowingradish.html

Hutchins, R. (2017, October 31). *8 Surprising Health Benefits of Gardening | UNC Health Talk.* UNC Health Talk. https://healthtalk.unchealthcare.org/health-benefits-of-gardening/

KJ Staff. (2020, November 25). *What are the Different Methods of Sowing Seeds?* Krishijagran.com. https://krishijagran.com/agripedia/what-are-the-different-methods-of-sowing-seeds/

Knerl, L. (2021, July 24). *The True Cost Of Growing A Garden.* Investopedia. https://www.investopedia.com/financial-edge/0312/the-true-cost-of-growing-a-garden.aspx

Larum, D. (2021, January 13). *StackPath*. Www.gardeningknowhow.com. https://www.gardeningknowhow.com/edible/vegetables/tomato/protecting-tomatoes-from-animals.htm

Leichty, C. (n.d.). *Are Raised Garden Beds Better than In-Ground Garden Beds?* Do Not Disturb Gardening. Retrieved June 26, 2021, from https://donotdisturbgardening.com/are-raised-garden-beds-better-than-in-ground-garden-beds/

Lobo, B. (2021, March 28). *Growing Tomatoes From Seed: How, When and Ideal Temperatures*. Dengarden - Home and Garden. https://dengarden.com/gardening/planting-tomato-seeds

Look, Z. (2020, January 31). *Every Gardener Needs A Good Rake And Hoe*. Hobby Farms. https://www.hobbyfarms.com/every-gardener-needs-a-good-rake-and-hoe/

Lussier, M. (2018, May 30). *5 Reasons To Grow Your Own Food*. Healthy UNH. https://www.unh.edu/healthyunh/blog/nutrition/2018/05/5-reasons-grow-your-own-food

Maggie's Farm. (2020, May 20). *Common Tomato Insects and How to Protect Your Plants*. Maggie's Farm. https://maggiesfarmproducts.com/blogs/bug-help/tomato-pests

Mantel, S. (2019). *Why are soils important? | ISRIC*. Isric.org. https://www.isric.org/discover/about_soils/why-are-soils-important

Masley, S. (2019, October 4). *How to Prepare the Soil for a Vegetable Garden*. WikiHow. https://www.wikihow.com/Prepare-the-Soil-for-a-Vegetable-Garden

Max. (2020, July 5). *15 Different Types of Cucumbers That You Can Grow*. Trees.com. https://www.trees.com/edible/cucumbers

Newcomb, L. (n.d.). *Remedy for Nitrogen Overdose on Tomato Plants*. Home Guides | SF Gate. https://homeguides.sfgate.com/remedy-nitrogen-overdose-tomato-plants-29733.html

Old Farmer's Almanac. (2017, August 12). *Soil pH Levels for Plants*. Old Farmer's Almanac. https://www.almanac.com/plant-ph

Old Farmer's Almanac. (2019, July 4). *Radishes*. Old Farmer's Almanac. https://www.almanac.com/plant/radishes

Palomo, E. (n.d.). *Do Cucumbers Have Shallow Roots?* Home Guides | SF Gate. Retrieved July 18, 2021, from https://homeguides.sfgate.com/cucumbers-shallow-roots-85473.html

Paul. (n.d.). *Different types of gardens*. Www.clausehomegarden.com. Retrieved June 26, 2021, from https://www.clausehomegarden.com/rubrique-concept/resistances-aux-maladies/different-types-gardens

Pleasant, B. (2019, March 14). *8 Tips for Growing Tomatoes from Seed.* Grow-Veg. https://www.growveg.co.uk/guides/8-tips-for-growing-tomatoes-from-seed/

Quinn, L. (2016, April 26). *The Benefits of Growing a Vegetable Garden.* Burke Rehabilitation Hospital. https://www.burke.org/blog/2016/4/the-benefits-of-growing-a-vegetable-garden/83

Reilly, K. (2020, April 15). *The Only Tools You Need to Start a Garden.* EatingWell. https://www.eatingwell.com/article/17068/the-only-tools-you-need-to-start-a-garden/

Rhoades, H. (2021a, June 4). *StackPath.* Www.gardeningknowhow.com. https://www.gardeningknowhow.com/edible/vegetables/tomato/watering-tomato-plants.htm

Rhoades, H. (2021b, June 29). *StackPath.* Www.gardeningknowhow.com. https://www.gardeningknowhow.com/edible/vegetables/tomato/tomato-fertilizer.htm

Sanderson, S. (n.d.). *How To Grow Tomatoes | Thompson & Morgan.* Www.thompson-Morgan.com. Retrieved July 17, 2021, from https://www.thompson-morgan.com/how-to-grow-tomatoes

SCOTT, T. L., MASSER, B. M., & PACHANA, N. A. (2014). Exploring the health and well-being benefits of gardening for older adults. *Ageing and Society*, *35*(10), 2176–2200. https://doi.org/10.1017/s0144686x14000865

Search | Garden Organic. (2016, February 9). Www.gardenorganic.org.uk. http://www.gardenorganic.org.uk/sites/www.gardenorganic.org.uk/files/MIND

Sedghi, S. (2019, May 16). *10 Common Types of Tomatoes—and What to Do With Them.* MyRecipes. https://www.myrecipes.com/ingredients/types-of-tomatoes

Sherry, D. (2014, April 25). *How to Harvest Tomatoes.* FineGardening. https://www.finegardening.com/article/how-to-harvest-tomatoes

Sigler, J. (2009a, March 24). *A Beginner's Guide to Fruit and Vegetable Gardening.* SparkPeople. https://www.sparkpeople.com/resource/nutrition_articles.asp?id=1292

Sigler, J. (2009b, March 24). *A Beginner's Guide to Fruit and Vegetable Gardening.* SparkPeople. https://www.sparkpeople.com/resource/nutrition_articles.asp?id=1292

Simons, L. A., Simons, J., McCallum, J., & Friedlander, Y. (2006). Lifestyle factors and risk of dementia: Dubbo Study of the elderly. *Medical Journal of Australia*, *184*(2), 68–70. https://doi.org/10.5694/j.1326-5377.2006.tb00120.x

Singh, B. (2021, March 23). *Sowing - An Overview and Different Methods of Sowing Seeds*. BYJUS. https://byjus.com/biology/sowing/

Smith, C. (n.d.). *Tomato Root Rot Due to Rain*. Home Guides | SF Gate. Retrieved July 18, 2021, from https://homeguides.sfgate.com/tomato-root-rot-due-rain-27887.html

Sowing, different types of sowing. (2017, July 28). Nature and Garden. https://www.nature-and-garden.com/gardening/sowing.html#

Stanborough, R. (2020, June 17). *10 Benefits of Gardening, Plus Helpful Tips & Recommendations*. Healthline. https://www.healthline.com/health/healthful-benefits-of-gardening#takeaway

Stross, A. (2016, January 28). *How to Start a Garden on a Budget*. Tenth Acre Farm. https://www.tenthacrefarm.com/how-to-start-a-garden-on-a-budget/

The benefits of gardening and food growing for health and well-being | Sustain. (2014, April 1). Www.sustainweb.org. https://www.sustainweb.org/publications/the_benefits_of_gardening_and_food_growing/

The Royal Horticultural Society. (2020). *How to grow tomatoes / RHS Gardening*. Rhs.org.uk; Royal Horticultural Society. https://www.rhs.org.uk/advice/grow-your-own/vegetables/tomatoes

The therapeutic properties of growing and gardening | Garden Organic. (n.d.). Www.gardenorganic.org.uk. Retrieved August 5, 2021, from https://www.gardenorganic.org.uk/therapeutic-properties-growing-and-gardening#:~:text=Mental%20health%20and%20well%2Dbeing

Thomas, C. (2021, June 29). *Save Money By Growing Your Own Veg*. Which? https://www.which.co.uk/reviews/grow-your-own/article/growing-vegetables/save-money-by-growing-your-own-veg-a8zg-Z4G3O3AC

Tilley, N. (2021, July 27). *StackPath*. Www.gardeningknowhow.com. https://www.gardeningknowhow.com/edible/vegetables/cucumber/when-to-pick-a-cucumber-how-to-prevent-yellow-cucumbers.htm

Unusual Urban Planting: 5 Different Types of Gardening. (2008, July 9). WebUrbanist. https://weburbanist.com/2008/07/09/5-different-types-of-gardening-unconventional-and-conventional-urban-planting/

Vinje, E. (2012, December 8). *Beginner Tomato Gardening Guide*. Planet Natural. https://www.planetnatural.com/tomato-gardening/

Boucher, E. (2022, October 9). *Raised Vegetable Garden Bed Prevent Dogs*. Vegetable Gardening News. https://www.vegetablegardeningnews.-

com/raised-vegetable-garden-bed-prevent-dogs/

Fruit and Veg. (n.d.). Scalpwood. Retrieved 3 November 2022, from https://scalpwood.com/fruit-and-veg.html

Garden Mantis. (2022, June 6). *Gardening Tools List.* https://gardenmantis.com/gardening-tools/

Gardening, I. (2022, October 8). *How to Choose the Best Indoor Garden Kit.* Indoor Gardening. https://indoorgardening.com/how-to-choose-the-best-indoor-garden-kit/

Gardening Tools Names: 35+ Essential Gardening Equipment with Pictures. (2022, May 2). Occupation Tools. https://occupationtools.com/gardening-tools-names/

Garlic Plant Temperature Tolerance: Ideal Temperature+Extreme. (2022, August 16). Nurserylady.com. https://nurserylady.com/garlic-plant-temperature-tolerance/

Growing Brussels Sprouts. (2020, May 29). Gardening Channel. https://www.gardeningchannel.com/growing-brussels-sprouts/

How to Grow Brussels Sprouts | Guide to Growing Brussels Sprouts. (n.d.). Retrieved 3 November 2022, from http://www.heirloom-organics.com/guide/va/guidetogrowingbrusselssprouts.html

Johnston, C. (2022, March 7). *Best (and Worst) Onion Companion Plants.* Growly. https://growfully.com/onion-companion-plants/

Max, C. (2022, August 19). *Who has the best lawn care service - LAWNNNN [2022].* LAWNNNN. https://lawnnnn.com/who-has-the-best-lawn-care-service/

Peas: How to Grow It. (n.d.). SDSU Extension. Retrieved 3 November 2022, from https://extension.sdstate.edu/peas-how-grow-it

Reaney, H., & Crow, R. (2022, July 3). *Onion companion planting – what to grow with onions to ensure a bumper crop.* homesandgardens.com. https://www.homesandgardens.com/advice/onion-companion-planting

Shiffler, A. (2019, November 21). *What you need to know to grow herbs indoors during winter.* Herbs at Home. https://herbsathome.co/how-to-grow-herbs-indoors-during-winter/

Sigler, J. S. C. (2009, March 24). *A Beginner's Guide to Fruit and Vegetable Gardening.* SparkPeople. https://www.sparkpeople.com/resource/nutrition_articles.asp?id=1292

What Tools Do I Need To Start a Vegetable Garden? (n.d.). Quickcrop UK. Retrieved 3 November 2022, from https://www.quickcrop.co.uk/blog/what-tools-do-i-need-to-start-a-vegetable-garden

www.ingramcontent.com/pod-product-compliance
Lightning Source LLC
Chambersburg PA
CBHW051829040426
42447CB00006B/431